I0456082

# Time To Crime:
# Doing Time,
# Listening To Crime

# Time To Crime: Doing Time, Listening To Crime

Michael Lee

Copyright © 2010 by Michael Lee.

Library of Congress Control Number:        2010909870
ISBN:              Softcover              978-1-4535-3226-3

All rights reserved. No part of this book may be reproduced or transmitted in any form or by any means, electronic or mechanical, including photocopying, recording, or by any information storage and retrieval system, without permission in writing from the copyright owner.

This book was printed in the United States of America.

**To order additional copies of this book, contact:**
Xlibris Corporation
1-888-795-4274
www.Xlibris.com
Orders@Xlibris.com
83224

# *Acknowledgements*

I would like to give thanks to the man up above for giving me
to create. I would like to thank my mom for the way she raised
and being there through my time in jail and continue to be her
To my sister and daughter for handling and taking care of my b
upon my release I still had a life. Other people I want to thank is
my brother Jeff for looking after my apartment, my ex-coworker
Vampire D, Ebony, Candice, and Rebecca for encouraging me to
lents. My friends Cristina, Kelly, Tony Rome (my best bud), San
unning my errands while I was writing), Chrissy (for checking in
omonique (who was my muse), Sharleeta and Teronda, and to th
met on Yoville and Facebook for the words of encouragement.

# *Prelude*

Click, click was the sound that radiated thru my head as the handcuffs were placed around my wrist. I was placed on the ground in a sitting position. As I looked up I glazed up tto see 12 Chicago police officers staring down at me. I hocked up a large clump of mucus and spit on the officer in the white shirt shoes. I was then picked up by 4 officers and placed in the back of the what we call on the streets a very large paddy wagon where I was the attached to a pole some how feeling like I was suspended upside down. The pain of the cuffs around my wrist and the pressure of hanging upside down caused all the blood in my arm to rush down my arm to my hand. On the way to the police station, which was only about 7 blocks away but felt like miles, the driver made sure he hit every pothole the city had to offer.

Once arriving at the police thru the back the door opened up and I was unattached from the pole and led out the back of the paddy wagon into the station. By now, the cuffs had cut off all circulation to my hands and they were black, blue and swollen. "Can you do something about these cuffs" I yelled to one of the officers, but was ignored. They just escorted me off the truck and into the station and put me in a big cell with a glass front to it. The ceiling was high and there were two metal benches that ran down both sides of the cell. Attached to the wall along the top of benches maybe a few inches above were poles for attaching people to, which they proceeded to do to me.

The cell reeked of piss and some type of disinfectant. The benches were cold and hard. The temperature inside was very cool and it made getting comfortable very difficult. As I sat there, the officers were looking at me as if I was some type of animal. I felt like a monkey in a cage. No words were ever exchange between thye officers guarding me. But guarding for what. I was in this huge cell, handcuffed to a wall, what could I possibly do or go. By now my hand was throbbing. I again asked if they could loosen the cuffs. One officer stood up, said something to the other officer and both approached me very slowly. I scooted down some, stretching my arm out to let the officers know that I was not a threat and that I was going to cooperate with them. "Ahh" was the only sound I made, as the pressure was release from around my wrist. The officer just stood there for a minute then they left out of the cell as a team of officers came in. Maybe about 5. One wearing a white shirt. I figured that this must be the chief or sergeant. He proceeded to ask me questions. "So are you ok?" There was no answer from me. "Would you like to tell me what happen?" he asked. "I don't remember. You tell me." I responded. He looked at me as if to get a different answer. But I knew my rights. I didn't have to say anything, especially since no one read me my rights. The officers got up and exited the cell. As they were leaving out, one of the officers yelled out to me "Take those shoe strings out your shoes." I looked down at my shoes and gave him a nod letting him know I understand. Once they left I sat there alone in this cell contemplating how I got here. When you are sitting some place in silence for a long time, many thoughts run through your mind. Mostly scary thoughts

As I lay there, what felt like hours, before the cell door open again. This time a woman entered with four police officers. She was a tall slender woman wearing a gray colored skirt suit, which really fit her body. She looked very beautiful as she crossed the cell to the otherside opposite of me and sat down. The officers stood around her as if she was a celebrity. She looked me as I sat up to see what this was all about. "My name is Sandy Jamison, the states attorney assigned to this case. First I would like to read you your rights" She gave her little speech and asked me if I would like to have an attorney present before we proceeded. I told her I would. There was a pause for a minute. I think she didn't expect me to answer the way I did. But for me it was a fear of not remembering what I did to get here that made me want an attorney present. I was never in a position like this before and the flashes of every law drama show ran through my mind. As I looked at her, her face, become comforting and she spoke "Ok while we wait for an attorney, would you just like to talk to me off the record about anything." "Like what?" I asked. She said, "About what happen to you. It would give me a chance to see if I could help you kind of sort things out." I told her I didn't know what happen. Then she started to explain to me what had taken place and what I was accused of doing. But I didn't remember any of it. To tell you the truth what little I did remember happening was totally different. She said that I attacked a police officer as he was writing someone a ticket. But I remember, vaguely, being attacked by several police officers. She wrote a few notes then she stood upto leave not saying another word. The officer exited the room after her. Again I was left alone.

After being process into the County's system, which I can only describe as Hell and given a rolled up bundle consisting of a blanket, two sheets, toothbrush/toothpaste & a bar of soap. I was led by a corrections officer, which I would later learn to call COs with a group of other inmates down a long hall, then shuffled up 4 flights of stairs to another long hall way. Along the corridors of the hallways were these big glass windows with a small office with what look like some type of control panel and an officer sitting in front of it. As the other inmates and I walk down the hallways, we were picked out of the line and told to enter the offices with the big glass windows. When my name was called, I stepped out of the line with 3 other guys and we entered through the door. Once inside I handed the officer inside the little office my two IDs that was given to me.

As I stood there, I could see beyond the office's window an enormous room about half the size of a high school basketball court. After about 5 minutes, we were escorted through the door into this area. There was two levels with 10 metal doors that wrapped around, what I would later learn to call the day room, like a square letter U. We walk through the day room to the stairway that led either up or down to each level. Walking through I observed two areas off to the left side, one being a washroom with a big trough like sink and a row of about seven toilets. In the other area was the shower room with about six showerheads. On the right side of the room were two sets of what I could only describe as metal picnic tables with metal stools attached to them As we ascended the stairs to the upper deck, I was escorted to the metal door where I would call home for the next two weeks. While the CO opened the door, thoughts ran through my mind. How did I get here? What will be in stored for me behind this metal door? Will I have a cellmate? Will he be cool? What will the inside look like? After going through the whole processing into the system that took over

10 hrs, I was pretty much exhausted and hungry. All they had given me to eat was two bologna sandwiches, which I still had in tow. You hear these stories about inmates taking your stuff and bullying other inmates so you put yourself on guard.

The CO opened up the metal door and this stale stench creped out the cell. The smell was of piss and old dust. When I walked in the cell I seen why. The room was dark with a metal toilet and sink attached to each other right near the door. I then realized why the pissy smell. Stepping into the room, I heard the loud slam of the door behind me then I notice dust balls swooshing across the floor. We must have waked up the inmate who would be sharing this cell with me, because he jumped up from the bottom bunk and screw in the bulb to the only light in the middle of the ceiling. "Hey what's up" the voice said, "My name is Kevin" Kevin? Is the thought that ranged through my mind. What happen to T-bone or half-dead, names that I have seen from movies of inmates names. "Nothing much" I replied, "My name is Mike". We shook hands. Relief is what I felt at that moment. Relief that this was a cool guy and that I would have to be trying to prove myself to this guy. Kevin was a 21 yr. old, about 5'9" who was a Moe (slang name for gang members riding under the five-point star) from the Southside of Chicago. He was a dark skinned brother, slim with a little muscle build. He did not look the criminal part. He was well groomed & very articulate.

After the intro, the next question, which no matter where you go every inmate is going to ask, was asked. "What you in for" he asked me. "Aggravated battery ", was what I said next. "To whom?" he asked. "On a couple of cops". His eyes widen "Really" he said. "Yeah." By his reaction, I knew that aggravated battery on the police was a big thing with inmates. Aside for murder, it was the most boldest and respected of crimes that one could have in jail. Mainly because every black man that's ever been harassed by the CPD (Chicago Police Department), wanted to take a swing at a cop. Some wanted to do even more.

Now as I made my bed I asked Kevin what he was in for. He proceeds to give me step-by-step details of how he was arrested. I was on the phone with my girl Tina. I call her my girl cause she caring my baby & she is the one who I spend most my time with & I actually love her. She goes to school in Indiana, so I don't see her as often. "When u coming to see me." Tina asked him.

"You know I'm on probation & can't leave the state. Also I have to go see my probation officer this week," I told her. "You were supposed to come see me last weekend," she said. "I know but my car been acting up & I didn't want to take a chance on my car stopping on me up there." I replied to her. "I'll catch the train up there next week," I said to her just to keep her from tripping & to reassure her that she is the one I love. "You better," she retorted back. "I'll you later," I told her & I hung up. I was sitting in my boys car at the time of the call to Tina, waiting on my mans (slang for close friend) He picked me up about 1 hr and a half ago. We had plans to go to this party to hook up with some broads. Once he got back in the car, we were off. While I was waiting for my mans, I rolled a fat blunt of Cush (A chemically enhance form of marijuana) & now we started smoking it. We were rolling down 120th street smoking when my mans sees some niggaz he wanted to smoke. So he proceed to circle the block to make sure these were the right guys. Then all of a sudden, he hit the gas hard as he pulled out his 9mm & let loose on those niggaz. Those niggaz scattered like roaches when you turn on the lights. I didn't know what my mans was up to, but that's my nigga & I got his back. "I made them niggaz scattered," my mans yelled out as he was laughing. "They lucky I driving or I know I would have hit one of them muthafuckaz" he said I was so high that all I could do was smile & say, "Do your thang nigga." We pulled the car over in an alley to take a piss. We were so high that we didn't notice the police car pulling up behind. Just as I finished pissing & zipped up my pants, I heard the cocking of the pistol pointed against my head. "Freeze fuck-face," the cop yelled out. My 1st instinct was to run, but the gun was already cocked & ready to be fired. And this being a Chicago police & me being black, he would have definitely shot me. I'm already on probation for possession of a control substance & with this charge, the gonna make me do the 1 yr an a half I got left, cause I violated it. They trying to charge me with shooting the gun because they were like how can he drive & shoot. They charging me with unlawful use of a firearm along with attempt murder along with other charges I know they gonna drop because they misdemeanors. So I'm basically fucked. "Yes you are, "I said

Kevin was generally a nice guy, he just hung out with the wrong people, in the wrong places, at the wrong times. We talked all night about his life. He told me about his girl in Indiana State University and how he should have moved down there with her and how he wanted kids with her but she couldn't have any. He told me about his hood and how even though he loves his girl, him and his guys kept the females in the hood around them. He told me about how he makes his living on the streets and how because of the broken home he came from, he had to chose that life. It was then I understood his plight.

Clank, clank, clank, clank, was the sound of the doors unlocking. A sound I would eventually get use to. I jumped up" What the fuck," I yelled out. "Breakfast", Kevin, answered. "Fuck, I just got to sleep. What time is it?" I said. Kevin mumbled "Somewhere in between 3:30 and 4:30 am." "Jesus H. Christ," I screamed out as I screwed the light bulb back in to the only light in the room. In the cell the windows had a metal sheet with tiny holes in them, so you could really get any outside light in and depending on which way your window faced, you could never tell what time of day it was. I was thinking to myself that I haven't ate breakfast this early since I was about 11 or 12 years old, when I used to spend the weekends at my grandma's house.

As the metal door open, Kevin went to the door and received first a little carton of 2% milk from another inmate, which he proceed to toss to me. Since I was on the top bunk, it was customary that the guy on the bottom get the meals from the door. He was then handed 2 brown trays. Kevin handed me my tray and I was like "What the hell this is suppose to be." Kevin laughed and said, "Breakfast. Food of the champions" We both laughed. When I stuck the spork into what looked like grits, I was able to pick the whole thing up. The grits were so cold, they formed into a gel like solid. I put it down then looked over into the next slot to find what looked like cut up bologna in gravy. Didn't taste bad, but it was also cold. So I gobbled it down with the 2 pieces of bread, drank the milk & juice, then went back to sleep.

Clank, clank, clank, clank, It wasn't shortly after I fell asleep I was awaken again. "Now what?" I groggily asked. "Court call," Kevin answered. "Shit what time is it?" I asked. "It's about 5:30 am." "Man I just nodded off," I said in frustration. Now Kevin and myself didn't have court but 6 other inmates did. The CO started calling out the names of the inmates who were to go. Court didn't actually start until 9 am for the majority of the inmates. I was thinking why are they getting these guys up so earlier to go to court? I would find out when it was my turn to go. So I laid back down and doze off to sleep again.

Clank, clank, clank, clank, was the sound that woke me again. "Oh fuck me, now what?" I screamed out as I jumped up. Kevin said that it was 7:30 am and time for us to go into the day room for 3 hrs. I was too tired to be leaving the barely comfortable confines of my bunk, but it was mandatory that both inmate leave the cell because some inmate had hung himself about 2 weeks ago so the rule was that no one would be left in the cells alone." Better grab your blanket,"

Kevin warned me. "It's cold out there" The CO opened the cell door and we came out on to the deck. I looked down into the dayroom and noticed there was about maybe around 20 other inmates some wrapped in blankets, others going to the bathroom or showers. I walked down the stairs, which led up to the upper deck cells and found a seat on the metal picnic looking tables. The TV was on and I thought to myself that it was a good time to find out the actual time. An inmate had turned the garbage can upside down so he could climb up to turn the channel to the news. As soon as he stepped down another inmate grab the garbage can and dragged it into the bathroom and used it to block himself as he too a shit. Another inmate was tapping on the CO office window to turn on the showers. This was now the time, I though to myself, to get the lay over of the place. See who is who and what is what. Therefore, I got up, leaving my blanket to secure my seat, and started walking over toward the CO's station. As I walked over to the glass to read the papers that wee plastered over the station's window I notice the activities of my fellow inmates. The other inmates were either engaged in over dramatic card or chess games, while other ones were engaged in extremely loud conversations. That's when I noticed the separation of the inmates. Most of the older guys were the ones watching the news or playing the games, while the younger guys were engaged in conversations about their street life, who they knew, drugs dealing, or the females they were fucking.

There was one particular guy that caught my attention. Never knew his real name so I just called him King Neal, because after every sentence he would use the phrase, "On King Neal." His conversation was like, "I got up this morning, On King Neal, I ate breakfast, on King Neal, I'm a drug dealer, on King Neal, I fucked this girl and that girl, on King Neal, me and my niggas be getting too high, on King Neal. Who ever this King Neal guy was, this brotha had much love for him. When using a term like the one he used, it's like away of trying to convince people you telling the truth about your exploits. Some people use, on my mama, on my baby's mama, on my kids, on my dead mama. Dead mamas always seem to be more to that person's heart, so either that or the kids meant it was very much the truth. This guy just went on & on the whole 3 hours we were out. Talking so loud that I couldn't even hear the TV or get me any sleep.

Clank, clank, clank, clank, I heard as the upper deck cells opened. It was time for us to go back into our cells. Finally, I could get some sleep. King Neal continued to talk all the way to his cell, taunting the inmates on the lower deck and actually getting into a war of words with a guy in one of the lower cells. "Get into your cell," the pretty female CO yelled at King Neal. She then came upon the decks and locked each door manually. Then the lower deck was let out into the day room. It was like opening the starting gate at Arlington racetrack the way the inmates rushed out their cells. The day room ceiling were so high up and there was so much empty space that wasn't fill, that every sound made in the room was echoed and amplified, so that made going back into the cell to sleep impossible. Therefore, I just sat there looking around the room. That is when I noticed how fucked up the cell was. The walls were dirty; the floor had dust balls rolling around on it, and the smell. "Hey Kevin," I said, "Doesn't this room look like a project hallway?" Kevin laughed and replied, "Yes it does". We laughed some more.

After a little while, a voice yelled through the little vertical rectangular space in the cell door, "How many in there. "Two." Both Kevin and I yelled back. Then 2 plastic packages of bologna sandwiches were shoved thru the slot. The package consisted of $ pieces of bread, 2 slices of bologna, bag of chips (some days), a snack (cookies, animal crackers, cheese crackers, or pretzels), couple of packs of mustard and one 50 cent artificially flavored juice. This would be the standard lunch everyday. So I ate and laid down to see if I could fall asleep again. Then of course, no, sooner than I fell asleep the doors to the bottom deck were open and the inmates went into their cells. I estimated it was around 2:30 pm. It was shift change. An hour after that we were due to come out into the day room again and once again I would have to listen to King Neal loud mouthed ass weave his, maybe true or maybe not, exploits. "Man I got so many bitches, on King Neal. Around 5:30 pm, dinner would arrive. At each meal, 2 inmates would be responsible for dispersing the food. They would practically fight over who was gonna do it if it wasn't for the Cos assigning inmates for the task, because if you hand out the meal, any thing extra you would get. Now dinner was a little more exiting to eat than the other meals. More food to eat and most of the times warm ad least. The inmates in the cells would get distribute their meals first, then the inmates in the day room would line up for theirs. Then it's like high—hell at a swap met. Like with every meal, there is always something you don't want that someone else do. This would start the constant bedding throughout the meals. "I got bread for a lunch juice, slop for a bologna sandwich, and cookies for lunch snack" would be the roars coming from the day room and even the cells. Shortly after we were finish with dinner, it was time for the upper deck to go back into our cells.

It was around 6pm and I was exhausted, so I prepare myself for sleep. I soon noticed that there was a vent above my head that was blowing out cool air. Now take in mind, it was the beginning of November and there wasn't that much heat coming into the cell to begin with. Me being on the top bunk, I was getting a full blast of it. Kevin managed to cover it up as best he could with the styrofoam trays from lunch. This would begin my 101 uses for the trays. This would become my routine everyday in Div. 5 Intake for the next 2 weeks.

The next 4 days were pretty much routine, except for the day Kevin went to court. That day I had to spend practically the whole day in the day room because no inmate could stay in the cell by their self until his cellie came back from court. Because Kevin had court in the suburbs, he wouldn't return until about 6 pm. When he did return, he had decided to cop-out for 2 years in the probation, which meant that he would be leaving.

About 8pm, that annoying sound of the door ranged out. "Kevin Woods, pack your shit," the CO yelled out. We said our good byes and I wished him good-luck, and then he was gone. Now I was alone in the cell and I decided to grab the bottom bunk. I laid down and realize that being in the cell with no one to talk to or with out anything to do was gonna take some getting use to. Therefore, I figure I could just sleep and look forward to the day room the next day.

Sometime later that night around 1 or 2 am, the doors popped open. An older white guy, maybe in his late 50's or early 60's entered the cell. I got up to twist the bulb back in. He threw the thin mattress each inmate gets, onto the top bunk. As he put the sheets on his bed, I introduced myself. He said his name was Alan. Alan must have just been arrested that day, because he wore some very good smelling cologne and the scent was still strong. Surprising, because of the 24 hrs. you spend in the district jail and the 8 to 9 hrs spend getting processed into the county jail. Once Alan had settled in, I asked the most asked question in the county jail, "What you in for." "DUI", he said. "But I'll be going to the joint in 24 hour, because I'm already on probation for a previous DUI. So I know I'm gonna have to do ad least 3 mos. off of that." Alan just didn't look like he should have been in jail for anything. Then Alan started to tell me about how he got here. I was a regional sales rep for a Starbucks coffee franchise for 7 years and was very good at my job. Nevertheless, due to downing sizing and my age I was let go. Then I became an inventory sales rep for White Hen Pantry, but then after about 3 years, they were bought out by the 7-11 change, so eventually I was let go from there. It's been about 10 mos. and I still haven't found anything yet. Not even, come close to finding any work. It's hard for a man nearing 60 to get work.

Well I had been depressed and having all this time on my hand with nothing to do, I start drinking more. The night of this incident, I was at a bar drinking. I know that I was feeling a little tipsy so I wanted to get home as soon as possible. I lived far away so I was kind of rushing to get home and not really paying attention to what I was doing. I turned down this one-way street as a shortcut. Cars were coming in the opposite direction blowing their horns, so I decided to turn off at the next corner, and almost hit a lady stepping off the curve. Finally pulling on to my street, I accelerated to get to my driveway. I pulled in my driveway and into my garage. I got out the car thinking, "I made it home". I was maybe ten steps from the door to my house, when I saw the flashing police lights. An officer had step out the car and told me to approach his car. Once to the car, he just looked at me and told me I was under arrest. Someone had given them my plate numbers, so they knew exactly were to find me. So now, I'm here and by this time tomorrow I'll be in the joint."

So in 24 hours, I was alone again. A few days went past before I was assigned another cellie. During those days, I pretty much kept to myself in the day room. I either tried to watch TV or sleep, which was hard to do with King Neal running off at the mouth. On this one particular day I notice this guy looking at me. He looked familiar to me, then I remembered were I seen him. He was in the bullpen with me during the whole processing into the county. We didn't have a conversation in the bull pens but I remember how informative he was. He was telling people how he had twice sued the city and won for wrongful arrests made against him. He was also telling this guy how he get his felonies expunged and where to go do it.

"Hey man, what's up," He yell to me as he walked over to the bench were I was sitting at in the day room. "Wasn't you in the bull pen with me during processing." "Yeah," I answered. "How long you been in this pod," I asked him. "For about a week. I've been on the bottom deck since I got here and they just moved me to the upper deck today because my cellie got bonded out," he said. Now Ricky was 57, about 5'6" and husky. He had served in Korean as a paratrooper. Because of all the jumps that he had made, he had bad knees and feet. Ricky was also a SD (Satin Disciple). He lived in a building his mom owned, with his 5-year-old daughter on the 2nd flr. His mom on the 1st flr and his brother and his 19-year-old niece on the 3rd flr who sold drugs out of his apartment. Ricky didn't like what his brother was doing because of his daughter and mom living there, also Ricky ran his moving business from home and was a recovering crack addict and it just made temptation even harder to deal with, knowingy that the crack was right there.

Now Ricky had mentioned his story several times while we were in the bullpens and I kind of over heard bits and pieces of it. Now he was going to tell me his story. On this particular case, I had just finish up some work for the day moving furniture. I move furniture for different furniture stores. I picked my daughter up from the babysitter and went home. Once home, I gave my daughter a bath, ate dinner, then my daughter and I watched TV until she fell asleep and I put her to bed. As I was laying down myself for the night, I heard a loud crashing sound as if glass breaking. I ran to the living room and I could hear a lot of footsteps in the hallway out side my apartment. I go to the door and open it and there was the CPD (Chicago Police Department). The Sgt. In charge turned and looked at me then said, "That's him right there. Get him." I was like, "What did I do?" However, they were not listening. They just grabbed me and pushed their way into my apartment. "What the hell is this about," I yelled. "We have a warrant to search your apartment." He said as he quickly flash me the warrant. It had my name on it, but had my brother's nickname. It was then I figured out what this was about and that's when I asked them could they be a little quiet so as not to wake my daughter. The Sgt. yelled, "Shut your mouth before I call DCFS (Department of Children And Family Services) on you and they take her away. They spent about 20 mins. searching my apartment and found nothing. "We need to get into the attic," the Sgt. demanded. That's when it struck me that the warrant was for the apartment attic on the 4th flr. "I don't have the key," I said. So they cut the lock and proceeded to search they place. While searching they came across some 45 mm shells and some old shotgun shells. This is when they told me I was under arrest. They were charging me with a UUW, Unlawful Use of Weapon, even though I wasn't caught with a gun or that the bullets wasn't found on me or in my apartment. Before they carried me of to jail, I was able to call my sister-in-law to come get my daughter. Now 4 mos. ago, I was coming home from work and they arrested me then for no reason, saying that they had a warrant for my arrest, but didn't have my name on it but my brother's nickname too. I'm out on bond for that case and now they put a hold on my bond and gave me "no bond" for this case.

Ricky then told me how he had sued the CPD because of false imprisonment twice and won. Ricky started telling me about the hood where he grew up. It was the same hood my brother hung out in as a youth and found out that we knew some of the same people who once lived around there. Ricky was generally a nice guy. He had lived his life the way he did as a youth, but now he was trying to do what was right for his daughter and him, but his brother seemed to be the root to him having that peace. I must to have heard Ricky tell his story about 15 times that day. I guess he had to vent his frustration some way. While we were out in the day room, new inmates came in. Ricky and I had spent a couple of days alone in our cells and he asked me if I wouldn't mind being cellies with him. I was thinking by his knees being bad, he would want the bottom bunk and I didn't wanna give that up. So I politely said' "I would do it, but you gonna need the bottom bunk and I just got use to it." He had already asked the CO, but when the new inmates came in the CO sent them to their assigned cells and one of the newer inmates was put in there with me instead of Ricky. Ricky looked at the CO as if he wanted to kill him for not putting us in a cell together. Ricky was cool but I was glad because Ricky loved to talk about his case everyday all day and he never let you get a word in edge wise.

Shortly after, it was time for us to return to our cells. Once in the cell I notice the new cellie making up the top bunk. I came in and just laid on my bunk. This guy looked about 27 because of the grizzly beard he grew without a mustache which made him look like a black Abe Lincoln. He stood about 5'9", medium build, and black as tar. Actually the more I thought about it, he looked like a run-a-way slave in the DOCs scrubs. I thought to myself that this guy looks like trouble and I need to establish that I ain't taking no shit. So I introduced myself. He said his name was Marcus. "Look", I said, "I'm a quiet person and pretty much keep to myself. I sleep a lot and don't like to be disturbed." He was like, "Cool, me neither." He jumped up on his bunk and I told him to twist the light bulb so we could go to sleep.

Later when we woke up, it was time to gout in the day room for the 2$^{nd}$ time for us. It was around 6 pm. Marcus at first sat near were Ricky and I was sitting, but the after awhile, I guess listening to King Neal talk, he gravitated over near him. That's when I said to myself that Marcus must be younger than 27. I didn't find out much about Marcus until we went back into the cell for the evening. After briefly telling him about my case, he started to tell me about his.

I learned that he was 19 yrs old, a Black Stone from the east side of the Southside of Chicago. His crew and he were some wild ass muthafuckaz in their hood. Marcus made his money writing bogus checks and through credit card fraud. He was a smart muthafucka and if the fucked-up up bringing and the hood hadn't taken over his life, no telling were he would have ended up in life I just sat back and listen to his story. Marcus had two main females in his life. One was Mexican-African American, Maria, who he had a 2 yr old by and the other one, Tamara, was all sista. She was the one he loved the most. She was pregnant with his child and due any day. This was really wearing heavy on his mind most of the time, because he wanted to be there when she had it. He proceeded with history.

I was at my girl Tamara's crib, kicking it with her. I had been there most of the day because I don't like being at my house because my mom be trippin' all the time. "Boy you ain't in school; you need to get a job and contribute around here." Or "Boy you here all day, you need to clean up around here." Well I don't be home long enough to mess up and when I do be there, I fill the refrigerator up. My pocket funds were low, so when I got a call from on of my mans about making some money, I jumped at the chance. He came and picked me up at my girl's crib. She didn't want me to go at first. But I told her will kick it later over her friend's crib, so let me make some money so we can have something to party with. When my mans showed up, I kissed my girl and left. Once I got into the car, my mans tell me about these checks he came up on. Therefore, the plan was to write a large amount deposit the check in a dummy account through the ATM machine, then withdraw the maximum limit which was $500. This is how we make our money. So on the way to the bank, we stopped by McDonald's to get something to eat. I spent my last because I knew we were finna make some. We wrote 2 checks for $1,000 each and go to the ATM machine at the bank of the person whose checks they are. We deposited the checks then withdrew the money. We were on our way to another bank. We took a shortcut down a side street. A police cruiser was coming down a one-way street at top speed, so we pulled over to let him pass. As they pasted us by, the looked at us real hard and kept going. As we were getting ready to pull out, the police cruiser backed up down the street and blocked us off. The cops jumped out with their guns draw. They made us get out the car one by one, as they searched us. After searching us, they started to search the car. Right up under the passenger's seat, they found some checks. These wasn't the checks of the person we just us but some other guy and one of the checks was filled out to my mans.

Now because the checks were found near me they wanted to charge me with the checks even though my mans name was on it. I was already out on bond for being popped off with some Hydro and my car got impounded. I was the only on probation, so I guess that's why they pinned the checks on me. My mans in the back seat was let go and my mans that was driving got an I-Bond for a $100 and was let go. Because I'm on probation, I'm stuck here. I'm about 6 mos. into a year, so I might just cop-out in court and take whatever the state offers. I know I'm gonna have to do the rest of the 6 mos. remaining on my probation, plus what ever the state adds on. But I want to be out to ad least see my baby born.

Now Marcus bond was only $1,000 and he claimed to have had buried $10,000 in the garage at his mom's house. He couldn't trust anyone to go dig it up. His family seemed to not care much about him. Practically the whole family was criminals or reformed criminals, except for his great-grandma who recently died. She was the only one that he knew truly loved him. He told me that he would give up all his family to bring her back. His mom had did time for murdering his father who was a street hustler, his grandfather was into check forging, his aunt was a crack head, and his little sister was just a petty thief. Moreover, he definitely couldn't trust his crew. He said he would just take his chances and if he went down for a year or two, ad least he'll have the money when he go out. The thing that tugged at him the most, was that his girlfriend was due any day with his child and he wanted to be there when she had it. He would call her everyday to find out if she had it yet. Marcus was my cellie for about a week an a half. When the CO 1$^{st}$ brought him in, I kind of knew he would be in the cell with me. I had this opinion of him as being another young loud mouth gang-banger. He turned out to be just the opposite.

There were a slew of characters that came in and out of Division 5 H—House. Some I got to know and like, but most I did not. Some liked me but most probably didn't or really didn't care one way or another, like I did. I knew some of their names, but most I didn't know or didn't want to know so if I had to refer to them, I would make up names based on their character, like King Neal. Now because I had been in Division 5 for 14 days without a shave, I had a full beard and little strains of gray was showing, so most of the young guys would call me Pops or Old-timer, like they did every older guy they didn't know their name.

There was this chubby young fellow, who must have though I was a repeat offender sat down next to me one day and interrupted a conversation between Marcus and me. "Hey old-timer," he said. I ignored him at first because of the interruption, but once I seen that he wasn't going away, I turned to him and asked, "What you need." "Do you know the law," he said. That's when I turned to Marcus and smiled at him and when he smiled back I knew he thought the same thing I did. Then I turned back to the guy and said, "No I don't, but what could I help you with." Then he proceeds to tell me his story. "I was kicking it at my boy's crib who sells blows. We were sitting around getting fucked-up and shit. I was there for maybe an hour when the police raided it. Everybody in there was arrested a charged with distribution of acontrol substance. Now my boy knows that I had nothing to do with selling the blows, so he's willing to write a letter to the judge telling them I had nothing to do any of the stuff they charging me with. My question is do you think that the letter to the judge might work?" I really didn't know the answer to his question, but anything is possible. So I said to him, "It will probably be up to the states attorney and the judge to decide if they will accept it." "They will accept it." He yelled out in an argumentive voice. "They have no choice cause it wasn't my crib or blow and my boy is gonna tell them in the letter it wasn't. In a calm voice I said, "Dude, if you know the answer to your own question why you bothering me with it." From that day on, he was know to me as I am the Law, because the first thing that ran thru my mind when he asked me Do I know the Law was Sylvester Stallone in Judge Dredd when he would say, "I am the Law". One major motto in jail is you don't back down. There is always someone that's not gonna like you because of there own insecurities and feel they have something to prove to themselves or their fellow gang associates or they just be "Player Hating". Being that jail is a gang-structured facility, if you're not affiliated with one, you are labeled a Neutron. This brought more problems, especially with the younger guys because they have absolutely no respect for Neutrons. It was like a 50/50 thing with me. Yes I was considered and Old-timer and got my respect that way, but I was a non-affiliate also which brought on disrespect, then because of the severity of my case it gave me respect, but then you got guys that want to try you then.

The next morning, Marcus had to go to court. "Good Luck," I said to him as he left out the cell. King Neal also had court that morning, but I wouldn't find out until later when the top tier came out to the day room. The night before, King Neal got into a serious shouting match with another inmate on the bottom tier. Marcus and I would call arguments like that "Lip Boxing" because they were arguments done thru cell doors with no real threat, but just screaming at each other because you know they are in the cell and you can talk all the shit you want because you may not ever be in the day room with this person. And if you did happen to be in there with them, they probably wouldn't do anything but holler at each other for fear of getting sent to the hole and in jail charges being added to the case you were already fighting.

The exchanged started over the inmate calling King Neal out over one of his "On King Neal" stories. The argument between King Neal and the other inmate got so heated that they had to remove the other inmates. Because he became enraged and was threaten attacking King Neal once they cell doors open to receive his dinner. What I found to be hilarious was the fact that all the shit King Neal talked about him being this bad ass, he was scared. You could see it in his eyes.

While Marcus and King Neal were in court that day, alot of the inmates were pulled out of Div. 5 and sent to other divisions in the county jail. Most of the inmates that were taken out of the division were King Neal's buddies, so when he returned he found himself alone with none of his cronies to surround him. He was standing in the doorway looking around and when he didn't see anyone he knew, in less than a minute of being in H—House he turn to the CO before he could sit and yelled out, "CO, my life has been threaten. If I stay in here, my life will be in jeopardy." All the shit he talked about how he was kicking ass in the streets and how he wasn't scared of no body. Now he didn't have his boys around to make him feel stronger, because they would have his back if he needed them, but it turns out that he was a big pussy, and that's on King Neal. I kind of knew that anyway, because in my life experience, I always found that the loudest person in the crowd was always the weakest too.

King Neal once tried to try me, but I wasn't pulled into his trap. I usually kept to myself in the day room besides talking to Marcus. People seem to gravitate to me for some strange reason; asking questions, wanting advice or opinions about their cases or just unnecessary conversation. One this one particular day, I guess he wanted to see what was so interesting about me. He came over to the table where I usually sit and sat down on the rails behind the bench, right next to me, on the side where I usually lay down when I'm in the day room. He did this just as I was getting. Now from where he was sitting, he started this loud conversation with one of his cronies who was on the other side of the room yelling his favorite saying, "On King Neal this, On King Neal that". I couldn't even hear the TV, then he asked one of his cronies to toss him the toilet paper that was on the table next to them. By him sitting so close to me, in the course of trying to throw it to him, it came in my direction and almost hit me. I swatted it down to the floor before it had a chance to strike me. Because of his placement of sitting, he couldn't get up to get the toilet paper, so he look at me as if I was gonna pick it up. I gave him a glance that told him "Yeah Right". He got the message and asked some other guy to get it for him. Then he tried to hold a conversation with me and I ignored his ass as if he wasn't even at the table. He got that message too. A few times his movement would become erratic and he would bump me. Now I don't know if it was accidental or on purpose. The first time I took it as an accident. However, after a few more times of this happening, I knew it was likely on purpose. It happen about 2 maybe 3 more times, so on the last bump I gave him this look right in his eyes. He was like, "My fault, Pops", and less than 2 minutes he got up and walked back to where his buddies were.

Now because of his pussy move, the COs had to put H-House on lock down for the rest of the day. Well until they moved King Neal to PC (Protective Custody) which took the rest of the day to do. This didn't sit to well with everyone because they look forward to coming out the cells to watch TV, make phone calls, take showers, or to have some human contact with others besides their cellie. I didn't care one way or another. Because so many inmates had been transferred, all the inmates on the top deck was moved to the bottom, including Marcus and I. Afterwards we just sat in the cell talked and played cards with the jail made cards. You have to love the creativeness of someone incarcerated. We used what we had to make due for what we didn't have. Milk cartons were cut up to make cards, the foam trays the lunches came on was used for shower shoes, toilet liners and writing pads, sporks were used as writing tools, hooks, and clothespins. The plastic around the lunches were used for storage bags for food. I would later learn more uses for other things.

Clank, clank, clank, was that familiar sound on a cold November morning. It was about 8 am when I heard my name and the words' "Grab yo shit". A lumped formed in my throat. What was happening? Was I being bonded out? But when I looked out the rectangular window on the cell door, I had seen other inmates coming out of their cells with their stuff. Then it was obvious, that I was being transferred to another division. After 14 days, I had gotten use to life in Div. 5 H-House. Besides, from the constant interruptions on a daily basics, the loud talking, which wasn't that bad since King Neal left, the cold cells, and cold food, I wanted to stay. It was just my cellie and I. We had became good friends who respected each other and builded up a trust factor. That was most important.

As I gathered my sheets and blanket, I exchanged info with Marcus and we said we would hook up on the streets when we both were out. We were escort outside of H-house down the hall where there were more inmates lined up on the wall. After standing in the hallway for 10 minutes, until all Houses had sent their transferring inmate, we were told to proceed down the stairs. The process of transferring wasn't nice, but it wasn't nearly as bad as the processing into the County. We were escorted into this room, were we would receive DOC jumpsuits. Then we were told to remove our DOC scrubs and put on the DOC jumpsuits. From there, we would receive our clothing from the storage. We were then given DOC jackets because we were going to have to walk in the cold to the new divisions we were assigned to. We didn't know where we were going. Some of the inmates were asking, but the COs escorting us just talked shit to them with things like, "Does it matters. You go were we tell you to." We were then handcuffed and walked over to a 2-story building. On the side of the entrance to the building the sign said "Men's Dormitory. This section of the county was Div. 2. It consisted of about 3 or 4 two-story buildings.

Once inside we were directed into a room filled with garment bags of inmate's clothes. We would then transfer our clothes from the bags they were in to the garment bags and hand them to other inmates for hanging. I would learn later that the inmates in charge of handling our clothing go through the garment bags of the inmates and take items that they want out of them. After that process we were given clean DOC scrubs, sheets, blanket, a towel, face towel, soap, toothpaste/brush, and a roll of toilet paper. We were handed the standard packaged of lunch consisting of 2 pieces of bologna, 4 slices of bread, and a flavored juice. We were then led to another room where we were told to get a mattress. Then we were to sit and wait to be assign to the house we would be going to. This was a process that took nearly 4 hours from Div.5 to Div. 2. While sitting there waiting, I had observed other inmates doing various odd jobs. I was tapped on my shoulder from a guy sitting be hide me. As I turned around, I was stun to see the face of the inmate. His face was swollen so bad he looked like an alien. "He man, do you have a lawyer you can hook me up with," he asked me. I said to him, "No. If I had a lawyer I wouldn't be hear." Later I would find out that he was involved in a fight with another inmate in the dorm room I was to be assigned to. It was obvious he had lost.

I was assigned to D-House: bunk 13. As I enter the dorm room and looked around, first thing came to my mind was the move Full Metal Jackets. The dorm room or house as it was called was about the length of a basketball court. To the left by the door was a row of 3 phones. To the right mounted high on the wall was a TV set which was off at the time. A few feet in front of the TV were 3 rows of metal picnic looking tables. As I walked past the tables towards the bunk beds, I looked to the left, and notice the restroom. The bunk beds were lined up in 2 rows, some on the left and some on the right. Enough beds to house a good 48 inmates. All the inmates were on their bunks. 40 something eyes on me as I proceeded to look for my bunk number. I approached the bunk assigned to me dragging the mattress and supplies, but there was someone in it. A voice from behind me said," We're not assigned to a specific bed. Just find one that's open." I was thinking, Hell I wanted my bottom bunk. Only thing available was top bunks. I settled for bunk 11.

I threw the mattress on the top and started making up my bunk. The other inmates just sat on their bunks, so I figured that is what I was gonna do once I was finished. The CO still had the door open to the house, but as soon as he closed it, the noise level shot up. Some of the guys jumped of their bunks and visited other bunks to talk, play card, chess, or checkers. There were different conversations going on about so many things but the one that caught my interest was the reason everyone was on their bunks. Reason being, they were on One-On-One, which meant they were on a sort lock down. Each bunk bed was considered like a cell with the 2 inmates sharing one were like cellies. During one-on-one, you had to stay on or around your bunk only getting off to use the restroom. The TV and phones had been shut off. Reason for the one-on-one was brought on by 2 inmates having a fight earlier, hence the guy down stairs looking like ET and no one admitted to the beating of the inmate and he wasn't telling either. This was some code of honor that I would never understand.

There were rules posted up inside the house that were created by the inmates themselves and if you didn't follow them, you would get banked out of the house either voluntary or involuntary. Some of the rules, not in this particular order were 1) Upon entering the house, you must take a shower. 2) Everyone must clean on the schedule day of your group. Group being your gang affiliation (Folks, Fin balls, or neutrons, the group I fell in). 3) You have to be in the house 30 days before you could touch the TV. 4) If you and someone have issues with each other, take it to the restroom, another thing they called one-on-on. 5) The order to line up to go receive meals: Fin balls 1st, Neutrons 2nd, and folks last. 6) When the lights are out, house is closed. Sunday thru Thursday. That meant no noise around the bunk area during those days because people had court the next day. 7) Stealing carries no probation, ment you got caught stealing you got dealt with buy the whole house. I personnel never got a chance to read the rules cause I'm not much of a rule person especially ones created by some gangbanging inmates. But since I wanted to stay under the radar, I pretty much used my one main philosophy, which was "In order to get along, you have to play along."

My bunkmate or cellie was a young fella you was builded and looked like Donkey Kong. They called him King, which I think was his last name. He was a Fin ball but never knew which gang he was apart of. Two days had gone by before I even said two words to him and that was only to find out what day the commissary came, which was Saturdays and where can I get a book to read. Division 2 D-House was a mixture of various criminals & gangbangers, old & young. There were Gangster Disciples, Black Disciples, Latin Disciples & Satan Disciples who ran under the 6 point star and was grouped as Folks. Then there were the Black stones, L'Rukins, Breeds, & Vice Lords who ran under the 5 point star and was grouped as Fin balls and then there were the Latin Kings who ran with the fin balls. Even though the Latin ran under different groups, they pretty much stuck together. The Neutrons didn't really hang as a group or have any organization. We were just there. Seem that there was always more Fin balls than any other group at any given time. Every fraction had there day to clean. Friday and Saturdays were neutrons days to clean the house. Even though I never moved from my bunk I still had to clean. I guess it was only fair.

Occasionally I would venture off my bunk to watch TV, mostly on the weekend mornings. Sometimes during the weekdays if something interesting was on Oparh, the View, Ellen, or The Tyra Banks show. Yeah those were some of the shows that the other inmates would watch. Weekday mornings, afternoon, early evens were pretty much the same thing, but the even varied. Then there were the games that were played on a daily bases like cards (cut throat spades & casino), chess, checkers, dominos, and copi-coo. Even though I always wanted to play jailhouse dominos, I had to pass because they had these made up rules and they gambled, something I wasn't interested in doing. Mingling with these guys I kept to a minimum. There was a few that I did eventually start holding conversations with, but mostly to either find out things going on or listening to there cases. The young guys were always very loud and disruptive. They were always ready to fight over stupid shit. "Who took my soap. Man nobody got soap like that", one young guy was running around complaining about. "Chill out man", said this one guy name Randolph. "I'll give u half my soap". After Randolph gave him a piece of the soap, the young guy still was complaining.

Now the older gangbanger guys tried as hard as they could to keep the peace. Mainly because keeping the peace ment keeping us from being one on one. That day I had went to court earlier and witness a fight break out over the authenticity of a pair of gym shoes. "Man these the real deal on these Nike's," this one young short guy was running around yelling about. "They the new air force ones." A tall dark guy from across the holding cell we were in waiting to go before the judge, yelled out, "Man those fake." "No they ain't, I spent $80 on them." The smaller guy yelled back. "That's how I know they fake cause they run $120." The talker guy said. "Fool you crazy, you don't know what the fuck you talking about. I got a hook up from my boy over there. He pointed to this Spanish guy who had just came back from seeing the judge with news that he was going home. "Yeah he did." The Spanish guy said. The taller guy yelled out, "Dude, all I fucks with is Nikes. I have a collection of them so I know what the hell I'm talking about. Now you could see the little guy getting agitated and with 3 other fellow gang members to back him up. The Spanish guy said, "Man I'm the hook up guy on shoes. I be giving out the good deals on shoes. There was a young guy who did strong armed home invasions sitting next to me got up and start to put the jumper cables on the little guy. Laughing and saying' "Man you gonna let this mark tell you your shit fake." You can see the guy doing the charging and the Spanish guy along with this other guy start to circulate around the tall guy. The tall guy came and sat down next to me where the guy doing the charging was sitting. The smaller guy along with the others started maneuvering toward him. I'm like, all shit here it comes.

Now about 15 or 20 minutes before this incident, the guy doing the charging and I got into a few words. He had gotten up earlier sitting next to me and this old white guy sat down. After about 5 minutes later of him getting up, because he wanted everyone to hear his story, which was: "Dude, I be doing these home invasions to make my money. I just go up in these buildings, sometimes following my Vics and when the timing is right, I just kick the door in and knock the mutha fuckas out. I then go about my business looking for money and jewelry 1st, but if I have enough time and depending on the situation like if I got help, we take everything worth some valve about. Only reason I'm here now is that when I had just did this job, I was walking down the street and saw the police. I took off running. I thought I had lost hem so when I ran up into my building they ran after me. I thought once inside I would loose them. I got to my apartment and ran in. Before I could get he door close they ran in behind me. Once they were inside and had me in cuffs, they searched my spot and found the merchandise I had stolen for the week and my pistol in the closet. Even though they found the gun in the closet, say they found it on me. So now along with the stolen merchandise, I'm also being charged with carrying a firearm"

Now returning to sit down again he saw the old white gut so he pushed him and the guy fell into me. I shot a look over to him and said, "Watch that shit." He look like he wanted to say something, but the sharp look I gave him he didn't. The old white guy gave up the seat and the youngster just sat down. He then started to mumble shit under his breath about him knocking mutha fuckas out, but I wasn't worry cause this wasn't a crib he was in trying to rob and I had already plotted my defense and was ready and he didn't have element of surprise. You see most of these gangbangers are pussies. They rely on trying to punch you (steal on you) while you not looking and having their buddies around when they start a fight to gang up on you. They will never fight you heads up or toe-to-toe. Even if they did, they know eventually if they start to lose their boys gonna jump you.

So as they guys started to approach the area were I was, I was thinking, yeah this fool might try to accidently swing on me during the chaos, so I got up. Besides as much as I would love to help this guy, but I'm not gang affiliated and if I get hit I'm gonna have to take care of my business and I am not trying to add a case to me. If you fight one you fight all. And that's just what the tall guy did. After getting out the way the short guy ran up on him and he hit the guy knocking him back then the Spanish guy ran up and he did the same to him. So did the home invasion guy. So they regrouped and attack all at once along with another guy. This time they were able to get a grasp on him, but he still was holding his own until the guards came in and broke it up. This is what makes life in jail on the edge. You never know when a fight will break out over something stupid. They pack these guys, who already are violent, in these holding cells, leaving them here anger and on the edge about their cases. Then when you hear bad news about your case, the last place you wanna be is stuck in a cell with 30 to 50 other angry guys smelling funky and talking loud. You definitely don't wanna hear about someone going home. I have heard guys trying to get shit started because they are angry they're not going home so they yell out lets fuckup whoever going home. Never seen it done but I have heard stories were it has. That's why you stay on your guard. Stay low-key cause when you stand out you become a target. But sometimes being low key doesn't help if you look like a victim. I told myself though, if I ever got into a fight, that I would fight to kill. Two reasons; one being you don't want someone or their buddies retaliating against. Two you send a message to the other inmates that you are not to be fucked with. Most of these guys know each other from the streets, but for me I know no one so I stand along.

An image is what gets you by. If they have an impression of you, you can pretty much stay under the radar. I had many image, so wherever I was, I just fitted in depending. Either it was because of my case I got respect or because I had let my beard, moustache and hair grow out I looked like a crazed old man. No one wanted to be associated with the latter. I was consider an old timer to the youngsters so they gave me my respect in that way and also because they seen me either writing or reading, especially the bible, I became like this guy to come to for information some of it spiritual. Don't know why this happen because I didn't know about half the stuff they came to me asking about. Some wanted advice about their cases. This was my 1st time being locked up so I didn't know anything like some of these other guys did. The guys I would dub jail house lawyers. These were guys who been in and out the system so much that they though they knew every thing about everyone's cases. When it came to them telling me about my case they had been 100% wrong, but they were able to give some people advice or relieve about their cases. As far as the spiritual guidance, this was the 1st time I had actually completely read the bible & understood it, but I wasn't no preacher. The County had those too, self ordain ministers or what I call jailhouse preachers.

Like I said before, I pretty much stayed on my bunk to myself. I just sat back and listen to the conversations around me when I wasn't reading or writing. Sometimes I had no choice because the conversations just got so damn loud, that I couldn't concentrate anyway. Most of the conversations were about what they did to get here, about how the case was going in court, about their life styles on the street (whether true or real) or about their females which they referred to as their bitches. "When my bitch gonna come see me. My bitch better put sum money on my books. My bitch better come visit me. My got a shorty by this bitch. My bitch knows her place. Out of the 48 inmates, I only heard 3 or 4 guys referred to the ladies in their life as their woman, lady, girlfriend, baby mama, or wife. Most of these guys were here on domestic violence cases anyway.

Returning from court with news of another continuance, I just wanted to lay on my bunk and chill to myself with my thoughts which was very hard to with 48 different conversations going on. These two inmates playing cards, in particular caught my interest. "Yeah man, I'm in here on possession of heroin. I got caught with 9 bags and they hit me with an intent to distribute." The younger was saying. The tall slender older inmate replied, "I'm I here on a domestic." "Where you from," the younger guy asked. "I'm from around 69 & State, but the little bitch I got the domestic on lives around 44 & Michigan," the taller guy answered. "For real," the younger guy said looking more interested. "I been hanging over there on 43& State for years and I know just about everyone around there. What's her name?" "Her name is Brenda. She a red bone with a nice ass body about 5'5". She stays in the brown court way building on the corner of 44 & Michigan. The older guy said. "Does she have a brother name Robert they call Rip?" asked the younger inmate. "Yeah" "Man you talking about Brenda stalls. That's my cousin the younger guy said. "No shit. Yeah that little bitch and I been fucking around for a minute. Her ass got out of pocket and I had to take care of my business," The older inmate responded. "I haven't seen her in like a minute, but I kicks it with Rip all the time," the younger inmate replied. "Small world, huh?" the older guy said as the two went back to playing cards. I was thinking like, the calling of his cousin a bitch had no affect on the young inmate. I just laughed to myself and rolled on my side.

Now I was facing the section of bunks on my left side, which was dubbed Little Spanish Ghetto because that is where all the Spanish guys sleep. There were two Spanish guys asking this other Spanish inmate about his case. His buddies and him had thrown this party were at the party they sold guns. The party had got a little loud and the neighbors called the police. So the party was dispersed. The Spanish inmate lived a couple of houses down, so he went out the back and put the guns in the trunk of his car and drove to his crib. As he was transporting the guns into the crib, the cops rolled up on him. He was caught with 12 different types or firearms from hand guns to assault rifles and plenty of rounds of ammo for them. What stuck me as being funny was that there was certain inmate who wanted to make sure they go his info so they can get the hook up.

There was a lot of inmates here that had bullshit cases, me being one of them. Not to say these fellas weren't already criminals, because they were caught, but because the cops involved probably stopped them for no reason at all, except for the fact that they were profiling. Profiling is when a cop harasses a person based on race, sex, or age.

Sometime cops harass people because they know them from the neighborhood. Cops know that, 9 out of 10 Blacks or Latinos that they stop, will most likely be engaged in some type of crime at the time they stopped them. Whether it be possession of narcotics for selling or personnel use, a weapon on them, just commit a crime, or have warrants out on them. Then when the do stop them and don't find anything, they will plan shit on them like guns and drugs, then make false police reports. This is why a lot of these guys get off on most of these cases. There was this one guy here who says he had just bought a beer and was walking out the store when the police grabbed him, took his beer and opened it up and set it on the ground, then arrested for having open liquor on the street. He was trading stories with this other inmate whose story was even more fucked up. "Man, I had just got released from the police station on 61st & Wentworth. I walked down to the store and brought me some squares. I spent my last on the squares so I was walking home and I got maybe 2 blocks from the liquor store and 5 blocks from the police station when the cops stopped and arrested me. They said they were arresting me for stealing a car and then they drove me to where this supposedly stole car was. It was a 2000 green Ford Taurus. It had a factory radio and a bad paint job. It had no special kind of rims on it. It had no value so why would anyone want to steal it. I told them I had just gotten release from the 61st & Wentworth police station. Showed them the release papers and the numbers on my wrist wrote with a marker. They still arrested me anyway."

Another inmate name Darryl, who I was handcuffed to on the bus going to court earlier today, was telling the steps leading to his arrest. "I was coming out this little corner store when the police rushed up to me and throw me to the ground. Now they did find my pistol on me when they searched me. I was thinking how they know I had a pistol on me. Maybe the security guard in the store saw it accidently and thought I was finna rob the place and called them. So on the police report they said I pulled the gun out on them. Now everyone knows had if you pulled out a pistol on the CPD, hell any police in the US of A, I would have been shot dead on the spot. I used to gangbang when I was younger but I ain't on that shit no more. I got a good job and a family. I only had the pistol on me because I wasn't familiar with the hood I was in."

When I got back to the County and was waiting in the bullpen, there was this old guy about 75 years of age name Ben, I was talking to who was telling me about his arrest. "It was about 11 o'clock at night and I was walking home when the cops stopped me. I had a 45 revolver on me, so they arrested me. They said they stopped me because I looked like a bank robber. I told them I was carrying the gun for protection because a week ago I had been robbed and that I had been hit on the head. I showed them the knot but they still arrested me." Ben told me that he had been in here a moth, but he was going home today because the judge had throw his case out due to the fact that he had proof of being attacked and that the gun was for his protection.

Now all the cases in here didn't involve innocent people. Most of these guys here were repeat offenders whose criminal rap sheets were long. Over the next couple of weeks while waiting for my next court date I would hear plenty. I started branching out a little more, actually being a little more social. I decided that I would try to get to know my fellow inmates and not to judge then all as criminals. Besides, I wasn't a criminal but I was here. One inmate named Randolph was a breed, maybe in his mid-30s. He had been here for about a year fighting his case and had some type of rank or status to where the younger fellas gave him props. He was more like an enforcer of the rules and he peacekeeper of the house. He was a stocky guy, most were if they had been in here for awhile or been in & out of jail, which he had. He had grown up in a youth home, which is consider a breeding ground for criminals, since the state don't really give a fuck about trying to rehab them once they are there. So once they are 18, the are kicked out and forced to make a living on the streets by any means necessary.

In the case of Randolph, he had been like the poster child. He had been to jail for being accused of murder, attempt murder, kidnapping, drugs dealing, and armed robbery, but you would not know that by talking with him. He was passionate about the raising of his daughter like I was and talked like he had good damn sense. He was in here fighting a possession of heroin with intent to distribute. "I had been riding around with this white boy I know for most of the day. We had been riding around doing our thang. I had stopped off to see my 18-year-old daughter at the store where she works at. I had my boy drop me off at the crib afterwards. My girl was there so I go bang her ass right quick so she want be tripping. Now everyone knows I smoke a little weed but they don't know I do blows. I tell my girl I'll be right back. Now they building I stay in, they are doing some rehabbing to most of the apartments so the building has a lot of vacant apartments in it. So I deip in this apartment on the 1st floor and peel me back one of my packs. I'm snorting and all of a sudden, I hear footsteps and walkie-talkies. So I stash my pack up under the sink. As I'm walking out vacant apartment, I see the police. He asked me what I'm doing in here. I lie and tell him I was checking the vacant apartments for the landlord to make sure no hypes weren't sleeping in them and doing a little touch up work in some of them. He syas to me that I was dressed a little to clean to be doing some touch up work. "Bring your ass here" he shouted out to me. I walked to him and he searched me. Now the white boy, this other guy and me, be selling our shit out in front of the building but we stash the shit around back, so it's not on us if the cops roll up. The white boy had left his pack out back under a crate with some stuff on over it. Now I don't know how or where they found the white boy and my boy, but they found the stash and arrested all of us. Now the white boy was let go from the police station and my boy had a low bond so he got out too. I got stuck. I just beat an armed robbery and kidnap case and now I'm in here that wasn't even mines and the muthafucka who's shit it is is out free." Regardless of the fact that Randolph was a criminal and had did some shit and possible a murder, that I kind of over heard that he actually did, I felt a little compassion for him because of the circumstances involving these case. Also because he really wanted to do the right things in his life but he was deal the hand he was dealt and he did what he had to to survive.

Over the weeks to come, I would see inmates come and go. I would get to know some and most I didn't. Like my 1st bunkie. All I really knew was what they called him, King, and until I heard his name being called out by the CO, I thought it was short for King Kong, Because that's who he looked like, a baby King Kong or Donkey Kong. That is how you were named if you didn't have your own nick name, you can best believe they will make one for you. There was a guy they called Quagmire for two reasons I assumed. One being he had a big chin and the other because his name was Glen. Glen was in the bunk next to me and for some reason he just didn't like me. Not like a gave a fuck, but it's hard to really stay focus when you got a mutha fuckas just trying you every day. Saying little smart shit or always complaining about every little thing I did which wan't much because I stayed on my bunk reading and writing most of the time. But for some reason he just had it out for me. I think he just was an angry guy that had some issues he needed to work out and maybe I looked like someone he hated. Maybe it was the fact that the case I was I here on was an aggravated assault on the police and he just didn't believe someone that looked like me was capable and wanted to try me. Who knows.

One particular incident, on one of those Saturday mornings when I ventured out to watch Saturday morning cartoons, glen and some other guy I never seen til that day started in on me. Now Saturdays was the day the neutrons day to clean the house. I didn't read the rules so I didn't know. I had been there a little over 4 weeks and no one ever approached me about this. It might have been due to the fact that I was always on my bunk sleep this early in the morning. "Hey ain't you suppose to be cleaning," Glen yells out. There was several guys up there watching TV and because my name wasn't called and I was into the Spiderman cartoon, I paid no attention. One of the inmates watching TV also turned to me and said, "Man, I think they're talking to you." As I turn around, the other inmate sitting with Glen yelled out, "Yeah, we talking' to you." "What you say?" I asked. "We said ain't you suppose to be cleaning? It's Neutrons day to clean." Looking around back toward the bed area, I notice several inmates sweeping. There was only two brooms that was assigned at the time, so I said, "Ok." A few minutes went pass, "Dude when you gonna start helping," Glen said in a loud tone." "There is only two brooms and both are being used, so they don't need any help now." No sooner than I said that, the door to D-H opened up and someone slid a mop and bucket inside. "There you go, now you can help," the other inmate said. I said in a frustrated tone Then another inmate walked to the front and grabbed the mop bucket, so I turned back to watch the TV figuring that since the bucket being used now there is nothing else to talk to them about. But they were still saying shit to me. "You need to get up and clean." I was like, "Why you guys so worried about what the fuck I'm doing." "Cause everyone suppose to clean," said the other guy. "Well I have seen people not cleaning and I seen no one saying anything to them," as I continued to watch TV. Glen asked who they were. I said, "I don't know any of these people's names." "You ever see me cleaning," the other inmate said. "No," I answered. "Have haven't ever seen you til today. Besides, I don't even be up here. Hell, I don't even move off my bunk." "You don't even clean by your bunk and you're up here now," Glen replied. The other inmate yelled out, "Dude you don't wanna clean we gonna have your ass banked. As I sat there watching Spiderman, which was coming to a close, my 1$^{st}$ instinct was to turn around to tell these mutha fuckas off, but I just ignoring them. Once Spiderman went off, I thought about the transfer over here. Since I didn't know if I was gonna be banked to another Division, and didn't wanna go through that processing of transferring again & the only way to get these guys to shut up was to use my philosophy, IN ORDER TO GET ALONG, YOU HAVE TO PLAY ALONG. Here in Division 2, I found myself saying that more and more. There was also an incident were this young guy was running around getting into it with people. He and another guy was getting ready to fight, but the CO caught them and they had him banked because he started the shit.

There were small confrontations with Glen and the other inmate who later I would find that he was called Boyer. I guess it was his lastt name. On one occasion he tried to front me off in front of everyone. "Dude you stink," and he just kept saying it louder and louder until his little cronies started laughing. I just ignored him because he stanked worst than I did. Thing is, the County was supposed to distribute clean uniforms once a week and they had not did so in 3 weeks. If you didn't have an extra one like most guys had, you were just stuck with wearing it 24/7. That means sleeping in it, going to court in it, & even after taking a shower put it back on. And if you didn't know anyone you could borrow things from or have money on your books for commissary to get soap, deodorant, underwear, even detergent to wash your DOCs, you had to walk around smelling.

The rest of that day I just laid on my bunk. I inmate next to me had went home that day and looking over on the bunk with no mattress I found a version of The New Testament. What drew me to pick it up was that I wanted to look up Psalm 23. Yea, though I walk through the valley of the shadow of death, I will fear no evil. Then I ran across Hebrews 13:5; So we may boldly say, "The LORD is my helper: I will not fear. What can man do to me?" These passages would help me to keep my edge in here. I knew what I was capable of doing if I got into it with a couple of guys, but in here I was severely out numbered. Because these gangbanger type guys never fight alone even if they are winning. Plus I haven't even worked out since I been in the County which was going on a month and these guys worked out every day doing basic calaystatics involving push ups and home made weights made out of garbage bags filled with water wrapped in pillow cases. I knew were my strength lie if I had to fight them, but fighting would just lead to another case against me and I not looking to be in here no longer than I have to.

As The New Testament became my new reading material, because books were hard to come by, it would open me up to the power of the word. I started of with Genesis because I always had this question about how if GOD create the earth and then put Adam here along with the animals 1st, at what point did the dinosaurs walked it. These words would become my shield to deal with the negativity that would encircle me on a day to day basic. When inmates see you reading the Bible or any source of spiritual writings, they tend to pretty much respect you. I had about 5 little confrontations, but since the other inmates had saw me reading it, the started coming to me for some spiritual advice, like I was some preacher. I would just tell them that I just started reading it myself and that they need to 1<sup>st</sup> read it to get their own interruption of it, but I was still able to give them some information that always seemed to satisfy them.

Now it's been about 45 days since I been in the County. I had finally gotten money on my books to buy some commissary. I had 3 court appearances and just received my Public Defender along with next court date that was to be 14 days away. I'm starting to get off my bunk even more now and due to the New Testament and guys seeing me write and draw, I had a little social group of my own. There was Youngblood, who was my bunkie before he was forced to move from the bottom bunk. Then this young neutron guy, who I never did catch his name, I just called him Casucus Clay because he looked like a young Muhammad Ali and had this attitude like fuck it, we all gonna die one day. Then there was this young Spanish guy in the bunk in front of mines, who I had given a halls to because he had this cough that would keep me up at night and Mongo, another young Spanish guy, about 17 years of age, who was in here for a home invasion.

His story had everyone laughing at him because he confessed to his crime and didn't have to. As I sat there he told me his story. "Yeah bro, me and my boy had did this burglary to a crib a couple a blocks over from where he stayed. We came in through the window after we found out no one was home. We were in there for about an hour or so. We found all kinds of jewelry and some money. We took the stereo, DVD player, camera, and video recorder. We got away clean and shit. After about 3 weeks the cops show up at my door. My pops was there and let them in. they told him that I had left my finger prints at a home that was broken into and that he were here to arrest me. I was fuckin scared Bro. So they take me down to the district police station. They want a written confession out of me. They kept telling me that I was gonna get all this time if I didn't sign it. Now I knew that I didn't leave any finger prints because I was wearing gloves and I never been arrested before to get finger printed. I found out later after signing that they had caught my boy. During the home invasion he had taken off his gloves at some point and had drank a soda from the fridge and left it on the counter leaving his prints on them. He had been to jail before, so he did have prints on record. I had confessed to the crime and they didn't have anything on me. He didn't even trick. They came looking for me because someone had said that he and I were close friends. So now I'm looking at about 3 to 6 years if convicted." Mongo seemed like a good kid generally and just did the burglaries for cash to have money in his pocket to be able to take his girl out and to get high (only smoke weed & drank) since losing his job a couple of weeks before the home invasion.

The other young Spanish guy, they called SD because he was a the only Satan Disciple in D-House. He was about 18 or 19 years old. His family was probably a little more well off than Mongo's family. Not to be judging men, but he was a nice looking fella and I could tell the ladies liked him. But he was in love and a one woman type of guy which I admired about him. His story went like this; "I was caught in my own house for trespassing. See my family had just sold the house and moved out, but we still had 3 weeks before we had to move out. The sign in the yard had sold on it tho. My parents let me stay in there for the 3 weeks. It was a chance for my girl and I could spend some quality time with each other. I also used it to bag up my weed and to kick it with my homies. On this particular night, I had some homies over and when they were leaving out the neighbors seen them and called the cops. They must have left the door open, because when the cops showed up, they just came straight in. I was laying down when they entered the room. They asked me what I was doing in here and I told them the situation. Because they caught me off guard, I still had some bags of weed lying around. They asked me if there was more I better tell them before they start searching. So I directed them to where I had the rest. I was arrested, charged with trespassing and passion of control substance with intent to distribute. My lawyer said I will probably get off, but unless I pay the bond of $3000, I would have to sit in here. My dad said that if they don't throw it out at my next court date next week, he would bond me out." Both Mongo and SD were good kids. Both were in love and they just only knew these ways to make money at there age. SD talked with me about his girl everyday.

Two other Spanish guy name Premo and Papa King, were cool too. Papa King was like the only Latin King in D-house and he had been here for 2 years fighting his case. He drew pictures for inmates who wanted to make their letters or envelopes that they sent home look nice. Sometimes also he would make cards for them. He had just copped out on his case for time, but since he had been in here fighting the case for 2 years, they gave him time considered served. He was awaiting to be transferred to a down state penitentiary, where he would dress in and dress out. Dress in and out was when an inmate was convicted but served the time in the County. And because the time was to be served in a penitentiary and didn't, the inmate would take the long bus ride down, be processed in and out, in one day, and not even make it to the actual inside. He would then have to foot it home on the bus with money that was on his books. What a bunch of bullshit to go through. Never knew what Papa King was in for.

Now Premo didn't speak much english, so what I learned about him was through SD and Mongo. Premo had been in here about 4 months, waiting to be deported back to Mexico. He was a funny, short crazy guy with a lot of home made tattoos which he did himself. He had once did 10 years in a Mexican jail for murder. You would never have know that because he was just always smiling like he was happy all the time. Running around joking and playing with the younger guys in D-House. He also was the go to guy for tattoos. I would learn about this by another inmate soon. I never found out why he was called Premo or what he was in for either.

There were guys who had been on the deck for over a year and were in nominated, through whatever method, to be representatives for the 4 different fractions. You had Randolph, who saw over the Finn-balls, Roco, who saw over Folks, Papa King, who saw over the Spanish guys, and Maywood, who saw over the Neutrons. These inmates were in charge of greeting new inmates when they arrived in D-House, making sure they read the rules, making sure they were straight setting up their bunk, kept the peace when different fraction had confrontations, and keeping the chow line order. See it was like this, when going down stiars to the 1$^{st}$ floor to receive our meals, we had to line up and the Finn-balls would line up 1$^{st}$, then the Neutrons, then Folks. If you didn't know where one group ended or know about the rule, they were there to make sure you did by hold the other inmates back until all the inmates of that fraction were in their proper position in line. This sometimes caused problems, because most Neutrons and white boys were the minority and was treated in such. We didn't have mandatory recognition among ourselves. So we never knew who were the gangbangers let along which fraction they belonged to. Then because, the younger gangbangers especially, they had no respect for us, they would try to talk to us any kind of way. This brought up another incident with another inmate and I.

When it was time for each meal there would be someone that yells out that the chow line was forming. I had started fasting the days before my court dates, so on this day I didn't get up to go down for breakfast. I would just lie on my bunk. Most of the guys around me knew that if I wasn't up already, I wasn't going down. This one inmate, fell under Folks started yell out, "You mutha fuckas need to get yall ass off yall bunks and get up and get in the line." There is a given rule that you never touch a guy unless you know him so he comes by my bunk and hits the side of it saying, "You need to get your ass up." I ignored him. He hit my bunk again and repeated what he said. I lifted my head a little and said, "Dude what the fuck wrong with you, don't you see me sleeping." Then he was like, "The line is forming and you need to get your ass up." I laid my head back down and said to him, "If I wanted to go down I would have gotten up. I'm not so leave me the fuck along." He just stood there looking stupid, and then he moved on. Few seconds later, I heard him harassing someone else. Then about 3 days later, when we were in the stairway going down to get our lunch, I was standing behind this on Folks, then the same mutha fuckas says, "Hey you. You need to get in front of that guy. The neutrons suppose to be in front of Folks." I just ignored him. Then he said to the guy standing next to him, "That stupid mutha fucka still haven't move up." I snapped my head around and said to him, "What fuckin' difference does it makes. He is only one person ahead of me. What am I suppose to do knock him to get pass.

I had court the next morning, so I just basically stayed on my bunk. That day was a day that would change my attitude about how I perceived the hardness these inmates was shattered. When new inmates arrived in D-House looking for the bunk number they were assigned to, they were told to just take the available bunk whether they were assigned a top or bottom bunk. Everyone just accepted it. But on this particular day, this new inmate came in and refused to just take any bunk. The bunk he was assigned was the bunk under mines. I was on the phone when the incident took place but the guy who was in the bunk was forced to move. Later I would find out that he had some gang ranking from the streets. Getting back to the bunk, he introduced himself to me. His name was Nate. We hit it off because he saw me reading the Bible and he advised some verses to me to read. I was like how can a guy with this much spiritual knowledge end up in here. He was in here on a simple possession of a control substance. Which meant he just got caught with a bag of heroin. He would become like this preacher of D-House in a way. Walking around quoting scriptures or giving words of enlightment to fellow inmates. It took some of the heat off me for awhile.

Going to court was always an adventure. They would come get us like 5 or 6 am in the morning. There were 8 Houses in Division 2, with 48 inmates in each. We would have to wait for everyone who was schedule to go to court. They handcuffed us together right-hand to right-hand. By it being December, we were given thin DOC jackets without any hats, gloves, or scarf. We would get marched over to the main building which was were Division 5 was housed. Escorted down to the lower level, we stood in the hallway still handcuffed for 20 minutes before they would then unhand cuff us and separate us according to where we had to go for court, thrown in the designated bullpens and sit until it was time for court. If you were going out of the County for court, you were pulled out the bullpen 1st about 7:30 am and escorted to the sheriff's buses that would take you to your courthouse. I had court at the County, so I remained in the bullpen until 9am. On the march to the County's courts, we were giving our bagged bologna lunch. The walk would take us a slight long walk underground to we came up on another set of bullpens. We were again separated according to the courtroom we were going to. We would sit until about 10 am, before being searched and taken to the holding cell behind the courtrooms.

I don't care which bullpen or holding cell I was in, the noise level was high. Everyone trying to out talk each other. As much as I tried to keep to myself, someone would always find a way to ask me something. Whether it be asking me about my case or asking advice about their case, like I was some type of jail house lawyer. Don't know why they always approached me case I didn't know shit about what type of time a crime carried. I had been to court about 4 times now and have been in many of the bullpens and today would be the 1st time I would see someone I knew from the world as we would say. It was Benzo. We called him that cause of his love for Mercedes Benz. He was a friend of my cousins and I had not see him in about 2o years. I really didn't recognize him at 1st because of the years of drug use he did had took there toll on him. We both kept looking at each other like we knew each other but wasn't sure until he came over and asked me what was my cousins name once I told him, we knew then. We chatted about my cousin asking the typical questions like what you in for. He was in on a possession of control substance. He had been caught with a bag of heroin. He was house in Division 9. That division was one of the worst divisions to be in. The gangbangers actually ran that division. We talked from the 1st bullpen we were in all the way to the County's courtroom bullpens where we then went our separate ways.

The Public Defender that was assigned name was Marcia. She was a sista who look mean ass fuck. She looked like she just didn't like anybody. Like when she came out to see me a week before this court date, she sat there with a look on her face like I just sleep with her a didn't call her back and now she was finna get her revenge. During the visit, I was able to tell her about what I remembered about the night of my arrest. She acted as if she didn't believe me. I said to her, "Are you on my side or theirs?" She was like, "What do you think?" I said, "I don't know case you don't act like you believe what I'm saying." She didn't say anything. So after we finished up, I left with the feeling that, I wasn't in good hands. So when I entered the court room she was laughing and joking with the judge and the states attorney and I was thinking this can't be good. But she was able to get my bond lowered from the $7500 to $2000. I went back to the holding cell with a smile on my face. I was going home. Then my name was called again to go back into the courtroom. My family had got this lawyer for me and he showed up late so I had to got back in before the judge and the Public Defender was removed from my case. The new lawyer was a legal aid lawyer so he was free. He came in and changed the court date a week after the court date I just received. Afterwards he came to the holding cell to introduce himself and talk with me. His name was James and he was an asshole. I told him they lowered my bond and he didn't believe me. He was talking down to me, which pissed me off. So once he left my spirits had been broken.

I went before the judge about 11 am. It was 12:30 pm before everyone in the holding cell had seen their judge. About 1pm, we were taken back down the same way we came up. Through the same bullpens. While waiting in the bullpen to be taken back over to Division 2, some young guys thought that it would be a good idea to steal some expensive Nike off a guy that was sleeping. They had one shoe off already when the guy woke up and was able to get the other one off before the COs entered. The guy was standing there shoeless not saying anything to the guards. They pulled him out without getting his shoes back. I just shook my head, because I will never understand why he didn't say anything.

The bullpens was the place were inmates from other divisions would be able to catch up with what was going on streets and to engage in releasing the stress of not having a positive court out come. I once heard a guy try to pump his boys up to jump on anybody who was going home that day. The way the County pack these bullpens and then have inmates just sitting for hour, you would thing they wanted fights to break out on purpose. You stuff 50 to 60 inmates from different gangs and areas of the city, with different criminal personalities, angry, frustrated, funky, tired, and hungry, what do you think is going to happen. They didn't care. All they cared about was just picking up a pay check. Yeah they would talk shit and make threats, but that was because they had a tactical team on stand by to back them up. I remember the incident I witness with some county sheriffs the day I came to the County. We had all just gotten there after spending 24 hours at the arresting district police station. This older guy looked as if he had just got his ass kick. He was bleeding from the head and was looking like he was finna past out. One of the guys in the cell yelled out to the guards saying, "Hey officer, there is a guy in here bleeding all over the place." The guard told him to, "Shut the fuck up before I come in there". The guy then said, "He look like he finna past out." "Didn't I tell you to shut the fuck up," the guard yelled back at him. The guy yelled back, "Damn man, I just trying to get this man some help. Next thing I bullpen doors opened up and the guard rush in and started punching the guy as he sat on the floor. Soon after that 5 more guards came in and told everyone to stand up, turn around, and put their hands on the wall. They then dragged the guy out of the cell and that was the last we seen of him.

I finally made it back to D-House around 3:30 pm. I went straight to the phone to call my mom and tell her about the lowering of the bond. She said she would bail me out tomorrow. My spirits were lifted again but were soon shattered the next day. The bond was still the same. I asked her to call the public defenders Marcia to find out what had happen. She had told my mom that because the lawyer James had taken over the case, she was no longer responsible for filing the papers to the clerks. And since James didn't believe me anyway, he never when back in there to find out if it was true. "That arrogant bastard," I said to myself. My mom called James and told him what had happen and he still didn' believe her either. He kept saying that ain't no judge gonna lower the amount of that high a bond to that low. All he had to do was call Marcia office to find out. Now I had to stay in here another 2 1/2 weeks before I go to court to ask again for a bond reduction. I was starting to feel really down. I had already lost my job of 8 years and was missing my family. I had missed Thanksgiving and now I was going to miss Christmas, New Years, and my birthday. I was saying to myself, all the praying and all the fasting for what. I was in a dark place now. This was when I really wanted to isolate myself. But it was hard to do when you share a room with 47 other guys. Nate had seen this and after a talk and a prayer with him, I felt better.

That night I would get to know this young guy they called Jordan. I thought he was called that because he was bald and maybe he played basketball real good. But would find out later while watching the Bernie Mac show that that was the Jordan they were talking about. Not only did he look like him but acted just like him too. Jordan was a book smart kid, who I figured out, did things because he wanted to be accepted. So as he started to tell me about how he got here, I knew I was right. "I was with my boy up North around Malden and Wilson. We saw this guy with an iPhone and I wanted it. Because I used to run track in high school and was pretty fast running, I mostly would just snatch and grab, but not this time. This time my boy and I, would use a system where we would walk down the street about a good 20 feet apart, to make it look like we weren't together. As my boy walk pasted him, he would turn around and follow the guy. Then as I was about to approach the guy, my boy would grabbed him from behind and I hit him in the face, knocking him to the ground. I tried grabbing the iPhone out of his hand, but he wouldn't let it go, so I hit him again. Then I heard my boy yell out 5-0, and he took off running. I really wanted this iPhone and figured because of my speed, I still had time to take it and get away. Police fat anyway and they wouldn't be able to catch me, but this guy just wouldn't give it up. I had started to focus so hard on what I was doing that I failed to pay attention to the cops approaching me, so they grabbed me off the guy. Now I'm being charged with a strong armed robbery. Because of my age, I was able to take a deal for 6 months of boot camp. That's what I'm waiting on now."

Boot camp was where many of the younger guys in here were waiting to go to. It was a part of the County, that was set up like a real army boot camp. There, they would get the same kind of discipline that was dished out in an army boot camp. Because there were so many young criminals, the boot camps were full and had waiting list. Jordan had bee in here 5 months already waiting. There was this other young guy that I would befriend named Mark, who only had to do 6 months boot camp, but had been in the County going on a year now waiting for a spot. He had been offered a year in the County but turned it down for the 6 months boot camp. With the year, he would have only had to do 6 months because of day for day. So now he was here a year already and still had to do the 6 months in boot camp. Boy the County really knows how to stick it to a person without vaseline.

Jordan had seen me writing in my pad and asked if I good handwriting. He wanted me to write a letter for him, but he thought his handwriting looked bad. I assured him his wasbetter than mines. But then I started showing him my drawings and he was so impressed by them that he asked me to design a tattoo for him of his girls name based on one of my drawings. He was going to get Premo to do it for him. I drew the image on his hand and he went into the bathroom where Premo was making the mixture of ink. The ingredients consisted of toothpaste, a couple of black checkers and water. Melt the checker pieces down, add water and the toothpaste, then mix it until it is black. For the tool used like a tattoo gun, they would use a staple straighten out, attached to a ink pen with tape or tied to it with string. At 1$^{st}$, I wasn't even going to go in there, but as Premo was doing the tattoo, he kept erasing what I had drawn on Jordan's hand. So I was there to keep redrawing it. A crowd started to form in the bathroom at this time, everyone wanting to see Premo at work. They started asking questions about who did the drawing and Jordan was telling them I did. This would give me a little more respect among some of the inmates.

Over the next 2 days alot of inmates would leave for various reasons either getting bonded out, shipped off down state or beating their cases and a lot of bunks opened up. A bunk in the second row up front had opened up and since this was a neutral bunk, so there wasn't any complains when I moved to it. As the day went by, the remaining bunks filled up. The bunk behind me and in front of me were taken by these two guys one named Lee who went by Anut and Buda. Anut was an older guy, thin with dreads. He was a little weird at times, but generally a nice guy. Anut was a follower of Hinduism. He was a homeless guy by choice that had a hustle selling liquid incents. He also told me about how he survived on the streets, which I found to be very interesting. He would dumpster surf around major chain stores like Jewel Foods and Walgreens. He said these places usually threw away some good stuff. Most of the food thrown away was always still in packages and they would throw out liquor too which he would take and sell to people he knew that would buy it. He said these stores also threw away general merchandise, like costume jewelry, sunglasses, and other stuff that he could sell. He would gather the items and display them on a table he would set up on the streets. He was trying to buy some crack and got caught on the same property were I live for trespassing. They searched him and found a crack pipe on him with some residue in it. So now, the state was trying to see how much residue was in the pipe and try to charge him with possession.

Buda was from the Southside and had been in the County for about a month. He was in Division 4, the workers dorm, during that time and was transferred over here because he had gotten into it with one of the kitchen supervisors where he was assigned to work. Buda was a little chubby and that is why Anut gave him that nickname. Anut would say Buda's build reminded him of the Chinese Buda statue. Buda came off as being a nice guy. Only thing about him that I found odd about him was his attention span. You could be talking with him and he would be listening, hinging on your every word. Then if he heard something else off to the side, whether it is another conversation, something on TV or someone getting into and argument, he would drift off, sometimes just getting up from listening to you and walk towards the new direction of his focus. It was almost like he had no control over it. Then he would come back over to me and try to pick up where he left off after what ever drew him away was over. Sometimes he would be in the middle of a conversation with you and then he would just blank out. The 1st day Buda arrived he would tell me about how he got here. "I was driving around with my homie, kicking it, getting high. As we approached 74th and Rhodes, the law got behind us. Man we were both dirty as fuck. We had weed on us and both of us were carrying a pistol. They hit their lights for us to pull over but we just kept going, pretending like we didn't see them, so we could have a chance to dump the shit we had in the car. We turned down this side street and pulled over. Before the cop's car even stopped, we bounced out the car and ran. I ran down this alley and when I seen that there was no cops behind me I pulled out my pistol and toss it on to this garage. I jumped over this fence and hided behind the garbage cans that were in the yard. I thought I had hidden well, but after about 15 minutes searching the alley, the cops came in the yard checking and found me. After they found me, they found the pistol. Even though they didn't find the pistol on me, I was charged with possession of a firearm. When I was taken to the police station, the officers were admiring my pistol. It was a 1819 45 Colt revolver. I don't really know if it was real or a replica. The cops were impressed by it. I am probably looking at 2 years if I lose this case. I'm definitely going to fight it."

The days just seem to roll by. The same routine every day, wake up at 3 or 4 am and go down to get our breakfast trays. During the weekday, after eating, if you had court, you would get ready. If not then you would go back to sleep. At about 5:30 am, the CO on duty would come in and yell out the names of people going to court. I would get up about 7 or 8 am to take my showers before the other inmates got up. Some days I would watch TV if it was on, mostly I would just laid back down to either read, write or sleep. Between 10 and 11 am, we would go down to get our bagged lunch. Now that I would be up it was either Talk with some of the inmates I had befriended or remain on my bunk doing me until about 6 or 7 pm. This was the time were we went down to get our dinner trays. Out of all the meals this was probably the most interesting to eat. It was always warm and the portions were just right. The breakfasts were all was cold and the portions were small. Lunch was basically 2 slices of bologna, 4 pieces of bread, mustard or mayo, bag of chips, pack of cookies, and a watered down artificial flavored juice. There wasn't any clocks around so other than the TV this is how I kept track of the day.

I was starting open up to more people, mainly because they were coming up to me. By now, I pretty much knew a little something about some of the inmates. The most they knew about me was I kept to myself, my name, that my case involved an aggravated assault against the police, the I wasn't affiliated with any gangs, that I could draw, and that I loved to read. It would start with asking questions about the Bible and holding religious debates, my drawings, listening to their cases, or giving advice about their girls, or general things. I now had people I could gets books from. Books were hard to come by in here. If you didn't have someone sending them to you, then you would have to try to get them from the social worker who only had a few and only came once a week. Reading the Bible was what drew a lot of the younger guys to me. I, myself was still just beginning to understand it, so it was refreshing to share what I was learning with them. Inmates always say that when they come to jail, it's for a reason. We never really know what that reason is or understand it but it is true. I became like a counselor in away. I talked with these guys and tried to give them a direction to go in when they were released. Mark was one of them that I think I made the biggest impression on. His religious knowledge exceeded mines, but with religion, you always have room for more information and a different point of view.

That night Mark and I 1$^{st}$ met, he approached me asking if I attended church. I told him no. I told him that before getting into a conversation about religion, one must 1$^{st}$ realize that everyone has there own opinion about it and the Bible. You get what you need from it, so it's a touchy subject. Mark just like Nate, came in here with great understanding of the Bible and religion, I just didn't understand how they were here. I knew Nate was here on possession, so it was obvious he got high. He knew he had fallen off the path and was embracing his time here. He knew his purpose, which was to educating the other inmates about the Bible. Mark on the other hand, I didn't know why he was here. He never really opened up about his case only just to say that he had anger issues with his family. I figured he was here on domestic against a family member. He and I would become kind of close.

Anut was weird but cool. He was always writing on what ever he could find, paper bags, asking for sheets of paper from me, toilet paper, and even the foam trays that came with the lunches. He had a plan that he was always working on. He wanted to pull all his resources and talents to form a group of workers to sell homemade jewelry. Everyday he would collect the foam trays and crave out shapes that he said were to become the templates for earring. He had garbage bag full of them. He wasn't the only one that used left over trash to make things. There was this older guy they called Papa G who made things out of the discarded chip bags. His two specialties were picture frames of different designs and baby shoes. You would be surprise at what you could use to make the things you need. I used the foam trays as shower shoes and as a writing pad before I started getting writing pads on my commissary. I used torn sheet edges as shoestrings for my shoes (they take you shoe strings upon entering the County). I used the empty chip bags and the plastic lunch bags as storage bags for food I wanted to store for later like bread, cereal, cheese, and sometimes the chicken patties and bologna, and sugar and jelly for trade. I would use the empty juice bottles as water bottles and to make a mixture of water and old soap to wash my DOCs. These wouldn't compare to some of the other things I would see. Besides the extraordinary way Anut and Papa G used items

There were inmate that used the ball from the roll-on deodorant to make dice for shooting craps, by rubbing them on the floor till they made the sides flat. Then they would just put the dots on with a pen. One guy made a small cooler to keep his juices and milk cold out of foam trays and garbage bags. Some used the foam trays as toilet liners. Old sporks and old toothbrushes were used like clothespins to hang our DOCs on the radiators to dry. I seen this one gut make a hairbrush out of a bunch of toothbrushes tied together. Toothpaste was used as glue to hang pictures or to write graffiti on walls and windows. Sheet edges were used as string for many things, making clotheslines, shoestrings, draw strings for DOCs when the elastic around the wastes lost its fit. Doo-rags wee made from towels, t-shirt, or torn up sheets. Then there was the way they made the showers private with a line made from the sheet edges then just throw sheets over it like a shower curtain. They also made a toilet stall by using sporks to attach sheets to the ceiling around a toilet. Some inmates made cards out of milk cartons. Also the milk carton were used to cook with. One occasion, the Finn balls had gotten a hold of some ground beef that was already cooked but just needed to be warmed up. They used my bunkies bunk as a stove. They lined it with chip bags with the foiled side turned up 1st. Then they laid paper bags over that. They then used butter from they breakfast trays as a grease coating. They would use expose wire to light a piece of tissue which was used to light a carefully put together stack of milk cartons. The expose wires could also be used as a water heater to make coffee or tea. There were other methods of cooking too. The exposed hot water could be used to warm up food by just wrapping what you wanted to heat up in plastic and then tying it to the pipe with sheet strings. There were also hot spots on the floor that got so hot u could actually fry bologna and warm up food.

There was also talent in here and not just the survival talents. Besides Papa G making picture frames, Premo doing tattoos, and Papa King making cards and pictures for other inmates, there were guys who braided hair and some that cut hair for the inmates as County barbers. Some knew how to trim moustaches, beards, and gave linings with the temporary razors we were aloud to use. Then there was always some guys rapping or singing. They had guys that were either human beat boxes or the tapped on tables, wall, and even their bodies to create a sound and snapping their fingers. You had your wanna be comedians, cracking joke on other inmates, the inmate lawyers who I dubbed "jailhouse lawyers" who probably could represent some of these cases better than some lawyers. They could tell you what kind of time your charges carry and what courthouse your case is gonna be held at by the area of arrest. Then there were the dorm preachers. I wasn't one of them cause I just gave my opinion when asked, but there was a few like Nate, who kind of force his thing on people.

At 1st I kind of resented most of these guys, never giving them a chance. Mostly because of 1st impressions. Because even though they had some talent, it didn't stop them from being ignorant most of the time. Sometimes the ones with the most talent was the most irritating. Most glorified the street life. All they ever talked about was the drugs they sold or did, about the women they been with which they called bitches, the street gear, the cars they drove and yeah lets not forget the violence. Shooting at people, being shot at, beating people up, and robbing people. Most didn't even have a deceit education but knew all about different measurements and were good with math. You had to be in order for street survival. You had to know how to measure you drugs and to count you money. They could tell you the make and model of cars, engine type, wheel base and rim type. They knew their guns also. They history of them, what type of people carried them whether it be FBI, CIA, your local cops or military.

There were some, who had school smarts that actually went to college. Met one guy that was majored in journalism. These were the ones that were bored with life. Some probably did things as thrill seeking as in the case of Jordan. Then you have the ones that like to have a little escape and just got caught up. Some were working class family men. But just laying back and observing things(what I did most of the time), you really see people for who they really are. You have ones who seek attention by being loud all the time. They talk 24/7 non-stop, cracking joke on people, instigating fights, and always talking about who ass they gonna kick but don't do shit. These guys are missing something in their life. Maybe they wasn't loved enough or had too much love. Whatever their issues were, they always wanted center stage. Then you had the deck leader types like Randolph. He practices keeping the peace in D-House. Everyone went to him when rules were broken or they had a beef with another inmate. Some just to be in his grace for something. He probably was practicing peace because of a deep closet full of skeletons. Every now and then those demons would come out, but most of the time you would find him in deep though or solitude. Guys around him, looking for his approval or to get a conversation with him were probably just regular ass kissers.

Then you have the guy that tries to fit in at any cost. Most of the time these are white guys trying to fit in so they don't get punked. Like this guy name Brad. This guy was a straight up character. When he came into D-House, he automatically started trying to align himself with guys he thought were cool. He started by giving up or trading things off his trays. He would show them his commissary receipt, stating that he had $100 on his books and that in the next 2 weeks he would pay people back. It had seemed as if he owed damn near the whole deck. He had other inmate ready to kick his ass because he started to become annoying being nosey and in the wrong area at the wrong time. He wanted to prove he wasn't no punk a couple of time which almost got him a pumpkin head. Only reason it didn't happen was because if he did get jumped on, he would get banked and all the people he owe wouldn't have gotten paid. So the guy was talked out of it. So when his commissary did come, he owed so much that he wasn't left with anything and his ass was thrown to the wolves. Then there was this young white guy name Mike, who I would refer to as a wigger ( white boy + Nigga = wigger). He wanted to be and act black so bad that he would sometimes make the mistake of saying stuff like "Wat up, my niggas" or "Me and my niggas", which almost got his wig split.

You had your crazy looking dudes, who looked like he just murdered his whole family, the weird quiet dude who keeps to himself, but did things I guess to amuse himself. You have your sleepers, who only will get up for the meals and use the washroom. You had your house nigga who make sure everyone was following the house rules and who was in everyone's business. Some of these people fit into multiple categories. Me on the other hand, I would describe myself as a social loner. I keep to myself, but people seem to like to seek me out for whatever reason. At times, I could come off as being and asshole because people would come to me while I'm reading or writing and interrupt me for some personal stupid shit or asking stupid questions. If I'm writing, "What you writing?", if I'm reading, "What you reading?", if I'm drawing, "What you drawing?", if I'm eating, "You wanna trade this for that?". I enjoy my me time to myself and just didn't want to be bothered by bullshit conversation. Some people just don't understand that. Oh yeah, I don't even want to get started on the begging guys. They will ask you for things without a conscious thought. They are probably the type of people you see standing in front of the neighborhood liquor stores asking for shit or trying to sell stuff as you walk by. These inmates will ask you for stuff before even taking the time out to know you. They be asking for pieces of your commissary food like cookies, honey buns, candy bars, and chips. Heck it's only about 25 chips in a bag and you want 5 of them. What is 5 chips gonna do for you. They be asking do you have extra mustard, mayo, sugar, or jelly. First off, I be saying to myself, I get the same shit they be getting everyday, what makes them think I have anything extra and if I did why would I give it to them, wouldn't I want to save it for my self. This inmate name Pop-a-lock, moved in the bunk behind me, They called him Pop-a-lock because he would pop-lock for people to get money. Every time I would get off my bunk this guy would jump up to see if I was going into my foot locker to see what I was getting. He would be like "Hey man, you have any cookies or crackers." Now he be knowing damn well I had these items in there, because he seen me put them in there when my commissary came. Now the 1st time he asked me, I gave him a few crackers. My cookies were like gold, no one got theses. Now you know the old saying about "Feed a stray cat and you won't get rid of him", well that applied to Pop-a-lock. Once you let him use something or gave him something, he would constantly ask for things. Brought that to and end very quick though. Just told him no. Most of these inmates gathered in social groups as men and not just as gang members. They found common grounds to develop these groups. It seemed that the groups always seem to have the same variety of characters. There was the leader type, like Randolph. Then he would have his minion types who probably would do anything he wanted them to. There was an instigator, a joker, a fool, a quiet guy, the CO boot licker, the young hot head, the sneak, the den mother type, the nosey one, and the loner asshole type, like me.

Over the next two weeks, Anut and Mark both had left. Mark finally got his call for boot camp and Anut's case was thrown out of courts due to not enough residue in his pipe. The time here, I think was somewhat good for him. It kept him off the streets during those cold winter days. We had exchanged information and he had told me about a church that he went to every Sunday to eat and gave me his brother's number. We talked about maybe meeting each other on the outside. Same thing with Mark, I gave him my number and told him to call me. Besides Marcus from Division 5 and SD from here in Division 2, these would be the only inmates I would exchange information with. SD I exchanged numbers with because he said he could get me a deal on a Playstation 3. The beds that they left filed up fast. There was the white boy Mike that looked like the actor Ray Liolta. He had a black girlfriend who form the pictures was very beautiful. Now except from him trying to act black was a pretty cool guy. His story went like this: "Me and a buddy of mines was standing on the block kicking it, when the police rolled up on us out of no where. I had a sack of weed on me. The cops were trying to grab us for loitering. I knew I had the sack on me so I pushed off from the cop that had me and ran. I had actually gotten away form them. So did my buddy. Couple of days later, they show up at my crib looking for me. Someone had told them where I lived. When they took me down to the police station the arresting officer said, "I have a surprise for you. Since you like to run and gave us a hard time, I'm gonna charge you with an aggravated battery." He said he did this because I pushed away from him.

There was a other guy that came on deck from New Orleans that moved next to me name Will. He had said that he was in here on bogus charges involving a retail thief. "I had just finish doing me a couple of blows and wanted some more. So I goes into the Walgreens on Roosevelt and Homan to steal me some shit to sell. I'm walking around the store and don't see anyone following me, so I goes for the Oil of Olay face cream. I get 4 bottles that cost like $8 a piece. I get these so if I get popped off, they really can't charge me with a felony, because the merchandise is under $200. That wasn't the case when I went to court. They charge me with the felony all right. They lied and said that the merchandise that I took was valued at $300. that carries 1 to 3 years but since I got priors I know they gonna try to give me the 3 years. But if they throw a year at me or probation I'm gonna take it." It seems like that is what a lot of inmate did.

They rather just take time instead of sitting in The County trying to fight and unwinnable case.

The last week before my court date was a crazy week. It felt like this tension was building up. There was a situation between Mongo and this other Spanish guy that was I thought was his friend. I was laying on my bunk reading when out the corner of my eye, I see Mongo all pumped up with his shirt off and socks wrapped around his fist. I'm thinking "hey Rocky". He was shadow boxing, warming up. There were guys whispering in his ear charging him up. I sat up and look to see who he was getting ready to fight.

That's when I noticed it was his homie. I had just seen the two talking and joking playing cards. Now house rule is, if you have a beef with someone, take it one on one in the bathroom. It never made it there. Hell, the never even fought. They were talked out of it by the older House leaders. It was established that they were friends and that the just upset right now and it wasn't any since of them letting other people charge them up to fight, when the were gonna be friends again anyway in the morning. They shook hands and that was that.

But unfortunately one fight did break out. It was more like the younger Folks trying to jump a Neutron. The way the fight when down was told to me by this gut D.L. "Man, the neutron Terry was on his bunk trying to sleep and the young folks were over there by his bunk shooting craps and being all loud. He asked them nicely the 1st couple of times but they kept at it. You know how they are when it's more than one. O they said something smart back to him. He sat up and next hing you know they had pulled him down off his bunk. Now he was holding his own against the 3 of them until he slipped and that's when they started stomping him." I think that's when I had notice that Randolph, again, had stopped the slaughter. So this one Folks that I always seen working out, who was built like Bruce Lee wanted to fight Terry one on one. But by the time the rule of having ad least one person of the same fraction in the bathroom during the fight and only them was decided, Terry decided that he didn't wanna go through with it. Again, hands were shaken. There were also more arguments over the vicious cutthroat card games escalated. In these games, they used either commissary or County contraband like kool-aide, juices, whole trays of meals, items off the trays and push ups on the spot, to bet with, which cause many arguments over what was of what value.

On the night before I was to got to court, there was an incident that involved basically the whole D-House. I was lying on my bunk, doing what I usually do, when I would here this one inmate from the outside say, "Southside is better than the Westside. Ain't no bitches out there, yall ain't got no grass in front of yall cribs, yall got a bunch of abandon buildings and it's dirty out there." Then this guy from the Westside yells out, "What you talking about due, have you ever been out west? Dude we got hella bitches boy and they be taking care of us. Them bitches out south only be thinking about what a nigga can do for them. Yall be shooting innocent as kids, you no shooting muthafuckas. Yall still on that gangbanging shit when yall should be that money thang." All the Westside guys started laughing so loud that I didn't hear what the guy from the Southside said back to him. Then the guys from the Southside started laughing. Now with both sides laughing, it was hard to hear everything that was being said. It was then that things turned ugly. They began to start shouting at each other, trying to over talk over one another and that's what cause each side to start arguing. There were guys from the same gang affiliations going against each other over this topic. I guess the pride of where you live, out weights what gang you belong to. I lived all over the city, but my heart was on the Northside. Therefore, I had nothing to say. Probably won't have said anything anyway if the Northside did come up. Not worth arguing over to begin with. The arguing got so loud that the COs rushed in because they thought the whole D-House was fighting.

After the noise had settle down I returned to my reading of the Bible. Like I said, it was the night before my court appearance. My objective was to seek a bond reduction. I knew that I could fight my court case better from the outside than in here. Plus I had had my fair share of being locked up, with a bunch of guys, 24/7. I wanted to be able to take a shower or bath when I wanted and not have to wait for the shower becomes available. I wanted to be able to sleep in my own king size bed on my nice sheets. I wanted to be able to eat what I want, when I wanted. I wanted to be able to sleep without people constantly yelling over my head, disturbing my sleep. No one disturbing me, period. Wanted to get home to watch what I wanted to watch on TV, watch my DVDs, play my Playstation, and listen to some music. But most of all, I wanted to see my family. I missed my mom and my daughter. They are the ones who seems to really have been affected by me being here. Since I been in here, my daughter has came to see me twice. Didn't want her to come at all because who wants their child to see them behind a 4' thick glass, having to talk through a small circular grate that smells of old spit. You can barely hear them through it so I would have to get up close and that's when the smell would hit me, so I pull back not really being able to hear again. Then after her waiting almost 2 hours just to see me, she would only get 15 minutes visiting time. Just her being there was heartening, because once I seen her, I want to reach out and hug her, but I couldn't and when she leave, I did't want to see her go. Then when I got back to D-House, it hit me how much I missed her and I wept a little.

I tried to get as much sleep as I could, but around here no one respect the fact that you have court. Yeah even though one of the house rules was on court days, when the lights go out, everyone must keep the noise down, especially in the bunk area. But you had the young guys up playing the cut throat spades all night and inmates standing around the bunks talking to someone one lying on theirs. I was nervous also or more like anxious to get this over with. It had seemed like I just went to sleep when the call for breakfast came. I didn't go because I wanted to get all the rest I could get. The whole going to court routine, is very tiresome. I had taken a shower last night, so I was able to get a little more sleep before the call for court. After going down being cuffed and walked over to Division 5 through the cold January morning, down through the bullpens and up to the holding cells behind the courtroom, I was ready for my day. My lawyer James came back to the holding cell to talk with me before I went out to see the judge and I told him that a bond reduction is what I was seeking today. He kept fighting me on the issue saying that the judge wouldn't lower it. That he been in the business for 12 years and he never seen a judge lower that amount to the amount I was suggesting. I told him that everyone has their own luck and that I had faith in my GOD that it will get lowered.

As I was escorted by the bailiff into the courtroom, I looked around and noticed that my sister and her fiancée were in the here. I would be directed in front of the bench were I greeted the judge. He would then ask my name. Then the states attorney would start to read off the charges against me. She was trying to paint the worst possible picture of me showing pictures of the cop I supposedly attacked. It was the 1$^{st}$ time I seen who he was because I didn't remember how he looked, because during our confrontation I blacked out. The James went it to his zone as he proceeded to talk to the judge about me. He painted the picture of me as taking care of an aligning relative and being a single father. He then he asked the judge if I could get a bond reduction. The judge looked at me and asked me how much could I come up with. I had talked with my mom and she said she could get about $3000 and this is would be the amount I tell the judge. After the states attorney tried in say she was against it, the judge gave me my request. I wanted to jump up and hug the judge. I was going home was all I could think of as I was escorted back to the holding cell, back down to the bullpens, the walk through the January cold air, all they way back up to D-House. Once in D-House, I immediately went straight to the phone to tell my mom about the news and to find out when she would be coming to pay the bond. She said tomorrow. It was around 3:30 pm when I called so I understood that it would take sometime.

I went to go lay on my bunk and get a nap before dinner. It was a long but victorious day and I just wanted to be left alone and sleep, but that I knew that wasn't going to happen. The white boy Mike came over to my bunk and started asking me about court. I didn't want to tell anyone I was going home because it was just something I wanted to keep to myself at the time. So I did tell him about the reduction but told him I didn't know when it would happen. After dinner I would very quietly start getting myself ready for tomorrow. Gathering up my yellow writing pads and other things I had collected over the 3 months I been here. I returned the books I had borrowed from Jordan and some of the other inmates. Then I took a nice hot long shower. After the shower, I just sat on my bunk and talked with Mike until I felt sleepy. Upon waking up fully the next day around 10 am, I called my mom again to see if she had paid the bond. She said they had just left fro m paying it. Now it was in the Counties hands and I knew it would take sometime. So I just made the best of my time until they called me. I had accumulated a lot of breakfast juices, lunch juices, sugar, state soap, deodorant, toothpaste, condiments, and still had some things left over from my commissary, like chips and cookies. I took this time to finish eating my commissary and past out the stuff I couldn't eat or had no need for. I gave Mike all the juices, sugar and the deodorant. The rest I gave to the person in charge of the neutron supply box.

At 2:30 pm, my ID was placed on the little window at the front of D-House. This was the way the COs let an inmate know that they were going to go somewhere. Whether it be court, getting shipped out down state, a visit, going down for your commissary, going to the library or medical visit and going home. I didn't notice it was up there until some inmate started calling out my name. It was so funny though. I had been here 3 months with ad least 30 of these guys and didn't none of them know my name or who I was. Besides Mike, Jordan, and Buda, everyone else that I befriended that knew my name had left. The guy just kept calling out my name asking where is this guy. He could tell how I looked because I had grown a full beard and mustache and my hair had grown. On the ID, I had a well-trimmed mustache and my hair was cut low and well groomed. Finally, he noticed me rolling up my mat and gathering my stuff. Now once again, I had been in here 3 months with ad least 30 of these guys not even taking the time out to know me in any kind of way, but now all of a sudden they want my shit. "Let me get your blanket, let me get your pillow, let me get that juice, let me get that toothpaste, etc . . ." I just looked up at hem and smirked, then hand my stuff to Mike, Buda, Jordan, and even Pop-a-lock bypassing them to do so. I pretended like they wasn't even there just like they didn't acknowledge me. I greet the people I knew farewell and exited with the quickness. On the stairway, I would run into Randolph coming back from cleaning up around Division 2. "You going home," he asked. "Hell yeah," I said. We shook hands and wished each other good luck.

I was asked to throw the mat in this room where the weight machines were housed and where they would set up commissary distribution and clothing change. I would then hand the CO at the desk my IDs and go into the room where our clothing was kept. There I would sit for about an hour until every inmate going home came down and changed into their street clothes. We were then walked over to Division % building and put into a bullpen until every inmate from every division that was going home came down. This would take another 3 or 4 hours. During that time, if you had money on your books, you would be issued a check in that amount. I had 37 cents left on mines and they actually gave me a check for it. Finally they would call us out 20 at a time while we got processed out by signing papers they had drawn up. We would then be led up to the 1st floor and to the window to pick up our personal belonging and a bus pass. It was about 8 pm when I walked out of the County. Even though I was a freeman, I was still bound to the courts. I was only out on bond, which meant that I couldn't leave the state or get into any legal trouble. Didn't have to worry about the latter. Because there wasn't any set time of release, I was force to take a bus home. It was a warm January night so I didn't care. All I knew was that I was GOING HOME!

# *Conclusion*

Part of our the laws of the constitutional states that, "We are innocent, until proven guilty". How is this law true. I just spend 3 months locked up because I was told that I was guilty before even having a trail. It was the cop's word against mines and they see the cops as being right all the time. If that was the case then why are so many inmates getting off on cases where the cops falsely arrested someone, didn't have enough evidence or never had any evidence against a person they throw innocent people into the County Jail, which is suppose to be like a way station for inmates going out to various state penitentiaries. Now if this law was true, then why is the County fill with so many innocent people awaiting trails cause they can't afford the high as bonds being bestowed upon them.

I could only sum up my time there as a learning process in two ways. 1$^{st}$ is the fact that being locked up with someone you don't know and being forced to share the most intimated parts of a humans life is not something I would care to experience again. Ever. Your pride and dignity are stripped from you the moment you enter the County. The guards humiliate you and don't respect who you might have been on the outside at all. Regardless of the seriousness of your case they think everyone that comes in there is a harden criminal and they treat you as such. They just don't know that this could be them. The second thing is that even though that I came into the county and average hard working fella with a good job that I lost due to the broken system. I say broken case you slap a high bond on someone that never been in trouble or arrested and you give repeat offenders lower bonds cause you know they are gonna fuck up on those bonds and then you'll have two cases to try them on. You hand repeat offenders probation like it's candy for the exact same reasons. Yes, I am be average in some was but I still know the streets. Boarder line thug is what this girl use to call me. I can hold my own around the white-collar types yet also be able to have some street cred. Being in jail I thought was suppose to be a learning experience in a more positive way. But to tell you the truth it's more negative learning.

I learned more about how to be a street criminal that living a productive life in here. I've met enough people in here, that if I wanted to, that range from drug suppliers to gun supplier to recruits for a small army. I can see why the younger inmates never change because once they enter the jail system; there is nothing or no one in here to encourage them to change. They come in here, see their friends, and feel like they are in the hood, hangout everyday and all night in here, just as if they do in the street. It's like a mini holiday to them. They make contacts in here to further their criminal life styles. This system is set up to keep criminals being criminals. There is no rehabilitation of any kind. Every worker there, is there just for a pay check. You have some of the COs and even the judges, who seen some of these inmates in and out of here so much that they know them by name. If you are one of the few that really want to change, you have to find some good people to align yourself with and PRAY FOR THE BEST.

# *About the author*

Michael Lee was born on January 10, 1967 in Chicago, Illinois. He has 5 siblings where he is the youngest of the 3 boys. He grew up in a single parent home, ran by his mom. The apartment was located in Cabrini—Green housing projects. For him it wasn't common to see violence everyday. He attended Lincoln Park H.S. He started working when he was in high school at McDonalds and dropped out in his senior year to work full time. At an early age, he wanted to take the burden of his mom. When he was about 19 years of age, his mom moved the family out of Cabrini—Green. At the age of 22 he moved out. He work for many years in various jobs always having longevity until he got bored. He always felt that there was something more he wanted to do. In 1989 he attended a medical assisting school, passing the course, receiving a certificate for it, but wasn't satisfied with doing that. On January 14, 1991, he was involved in a serious car accident where he fractured his C 6 section of the spinal cord that for 2 months left him partly paralyzed. Three month after his stint in the hospital, he would start working at a hospital in the food service department for 8 years and in 1998, he went back to school to get his G.E.D. After leaving the hospital in 1999 to pursue a different line of work, he bounced around awhile until he landed a job in a small hotel. Then in 2000, he attended a trade school for electrical maintenance and in 2001 finished. Also in 2001, he left the small hotel to go work for a newly build 5 star hotel. There the world would open up to him. There he would meet people who were passionate about using their talents to follow their dreams. Here he found out he had a talent for coming up with interesting stories and wanted to pursue it, but the exalting demand of work kept him from it.

On November 3, 2008, he had a life changing experience. He would get into an altercation with the Chicago police, which would lead to his arrest and incarceration for 3 months in the Cook County Jail. During his time awaiting his trail, he would become a changed man. He would strengthen the faith he flirted with for years. During his stay he would learn about the nature of criminals, about the inter workings of the judicial system and about himself. While there decided to write about his experience.

He beat his case on August 24th, 2009. Upon being released he decide that writing is what he wanted to do and has every since been trying to purse it. Time To Crime: Doing Time, Listen To Crime is his first attempt at writing and he prays it's not his last.

www.ingramcontent.com/pod-product-compliance
Lightning Source LLC
Chambersburg PA
CBHW020402290526
45785CB00005B/2413